venue

an international literary magazine

loved & lost

4

1999

Venue is published four times a year.
ISBN 90-5701-162-X
ISSN 1027-0272

Subscriptions and inquiries should be addressed to **International Publishers Distributor** in care of one of the addresses below:

P.O. Box 32160
Newark, NJ 07102 USA
Telephone: 1-800-545-8398
Fax: 973-643-7676

IPD Marketing Services
P.O. Box 310
Queen's House, Don Road
St. Helier, Jersey
Channel Islands JE4 OTH
Telephone: 44(0)118-956-0080
Fax: 44(0)118-956-8211

Kent Ridge, PO Box 1180
Singapore 911106
Republic of Singapore
Telephone: 65 741-6933
Fax: 65 741-6922

Yohan Western Publications
    Distribution Agency
3-14-9, Okubo, Shinjuku-ku
Tokyo 169, Japan
Telephone: 81 3 3208-0186
Fax: 81 3 3208 5308

Subscription rate:
One year (four issues):
    US $38.00
    GB £26.00
    ECU 32.00

EDITOR
John Brenkman

ASSOCIATE EDITOR
Bridgett M. Davis

CONTRIBUTING EDITORS

Hugo Achugar	*Carla Kaplan*
Michael Anania	*Wayne Koestenbaum*
K. Anthony Appiah	*Leo Ou-fan Lee*
David Bathrick	*Anne McClintock*
Michael Eric Dyson	*Rubén Martínez*
Farah Jasmine Griffin	*Gregory Rabassa*
Jessica Hagedorn	*Alisa Solomon*
Hannan Hever	*Jianying Zha*

DESIGN DIRECTOR: *Terry Berkowitz*

EDITORIAL ASSISTANTS:
Marianne Guénot, Hélène Poulet, Jung-wan Wu

EDITORIAL CORRESPONDENCE:
VENUE, 151 E 25, New York, NY 10010

Unsolicited manuscripts — FICTION and ESSAYS — are welcomed. Manuscripts should be typed and double spaced and will not be returned unless accompanied by a stamped, self-addressed envelope. Submission will be taken to imply that the manuscript has never been published previously in any form and has not been simultaneously offered to any other publication. We do not accept unsolicited submissions for the FORUM.

DESIGN BY: *Terry Berkowitz*

Contents

FICTION

Paris Trance

Geoff Dyer

A FEW DAYS LATER HE MOVED INTO HER APARTMENT. Luke's only concern about this change in circumstances was that he now had little or no chance of protecting his property. Nicole had a knack of filling her apartment and life with things that delighted Luke — love someone, love their possessions had become something of a motto for him — and there were times when Luke would see her spectacle case (i.e. her wallet) or her red string shopping bag, or one of her hats or shoes lying on the floor of her apartment and be so overcome with love for her that he felt like weeping. They were *her* things. Everything she touched became suffused with her personality. Nicole herself was aware of this capacity she had to lay claim to objects.

'I only need to have something for two minutes and it's completely mine,' she said to Luke as they unpacked his few belongings.

'You mean it's completely broken. Broken or lost.'

'That's not true.'

'Robust objects become fragile. Immovable objects disappear.'

'That's not true.'

'It is actually. What about my sunglasses that you borrowed two days ago?'

'I haven't broken them.'

'No. And the reason for that is that you lost them before you had a chance to break them.'

'They're not lost. I just mislaid them.'

'No, you *lost* them. Mislaid means you know where they are but you can't put your finger on them.'

'Exactly. I've mislaid them somewhere in the city.'

THE DAYS GREW SHORTER. IT BECAME COLD. As promised, the photographer mailed a print of the picture of the demonstration which they framed and put on the wall. Nicole was finishing her studies and had begun applying for jobs. With Christmas deadlines looming the warehouse became busier than it had for months. Lazare was under a lot of pressure and therefore happy. Luke and Alex worked late. The flu season started. Nicole stayed in bed for three days, coughing constantly. At nights the sheets became so drenched and cold with her sweat that they had to get up and change them. Luke resigned himself to catching Nicole's flu and as soon as she felt well enough to get up he began to feel lousy. He still felt bad when he felt better. Alex avoided flu but went down with a cold that at any other time of the year would have passed for flu. Sahra remained healthy, which was fortunate because there was a sudden rush of well-paid interpreting jobs. Christmas decorations went up on rue de la Roquette. A series of power cuts left the quartier in freezing darkness. It was too cold to play football. Sealed in against the weather, cafés became intolerably smoky — even more intolerably smoky than they were the rest of the time. Lazare decided to throw an impromptu — and somewhat premature — Christmas party. We all had to come, he said, and in the unlikely event of any of us having girlfriends or wives they should 'get drunk at my expense too.' Nicole, Sahra and Sally came and were all shocked by Lazare — shocked, that is, by how charming he was. In the presence of women his belligerence was transformed into equally extravagant courtesy. Luke's friend Miles came too, and some other pals of Lazare's. Everyone got drunk and danced and went away happy and those of us who worked there came back the next day, hung over, and cleaned everything up.

The Cassavetes season had finished months ago but an Antonioni season had just begun. The four friends went to see every film, too stunned by boredom and color and space even to consider leaving. In the black and white films there was no color to be seen, just the space and the boredom and people saying things. Some of what was said was lost on Luke because the dialogue was often in Italian and the subtitles in French. They were all in love with Monica Vitti, especially her green dress in *Red Desert*. Nicole liked the way the photos in *Blow Up* became clearer as they were enlarged.

'That was amazing,' said Luke when they came out of *L'Avventura*.

'Amazingly boring, you mean?' said Sahra.

'Yes, exactly.'

AT WEEKENDS THEY WENT DANCING. Luke, Sahra and Alex took Ecstasy. Nicole didn't want to and this became an issue between her and Luke. Nicole was adamant that she did not need to take drugs in order to enjoy anything. She was happy to get stoned — which she had done only occasionally before meeting Luke — but she drew the line at anything chemical.

'That's so stupid, Nicole,' said Luke. 'Dancing is much better if you take E.'

'But I love dancing anyway.'

'That's not the point. The point is that everything can always be improved.'

'How can you ever be happy if you think that?'

'How can you ever be happy if you don't?'

'What does *that* mean?'

'It means everything can always be improved by drugs. It's just a question of fitting the substance to the activity in question. Or finding the right activity for the substance. You admit that listening to music is much better if you're stoned, right? And dancing is much better if you take — '

'For you, yes.'

'For everyone.'

'But I don't *want* to take it. I don't try to persuade you not to. So why do you try to persuade me to?'

'Because you are missing out on something great. It can get to the point where there's nothing but lights and music. You can feel yourself dissolving as an individual. You can feel yourself not existing.'

'I love my existence.'

'And we could do all that kissy-feely stuff you see people doing.'

'We can do that anyway,' said Nicole. 'We can do it now if you like.'

EVENTUALLY NICOLE WAS PERSUADED — BY SAHRA, who loved it — to try a half when they went to their favorite club, The Coast, as this near-derelict space bizarrely called itself.

The evening began at the cinema. *Strange Days* was showing and, as the lights went down, the four of them passed the bucket-sized Coca-Cola — 'small' by the gigantic standards of refreshment — along the row and swallowed their pills. Luke had seen the movie twice before but this time it blew his mind, totally. Coming up, he began to feel — in the film's millennial argot — like he was wire-tripping, not so much seeing the film as jacking into it, living the experience of a movie which was a commentary on all the movies it had come out of: a pastiche of everything, even itself. Oh, it was perfect, perfect as the playback of Faith in her T-shirt and black bikini bottoms, teaching Lenny Nero how to roller-blade, and then heading back to the apartment and undressing in front of him. 'So,' she says, 'you want to watch or you going to do?' And Nero, sitting in his lousy apartment, looped into the past, feels and hears and sees himself say, 'Watch and see.' 'I love your eyes, Lenny,' she says, moving beneath him. 'I love the way they see.'

The apocalyptic party at the end of the film made them so desperate to get to the club they practically ran there. As soon as they checked their coats they were like dogs let off a leash. The dance floor was crowded, the music pumping. With every track the surge of the music deepened. The lights poured into their faces. Under Nicole's tuition Luke's dancing had improved to the extent that he was no longer, in Alex's words, 'quite the embarrassment he used to be.' If it still seemed like he was having a seizure it was at least a rhythmic one. Luke looked at Nicole and Sahra. They had their arms round each other, laughing. Sahra moved over to Alex and they began dancing together. Nicole danced over to Luke and kissed him. She was wearing a sleeveless white dress, plimsolls. Her eyes were wet with laughter. Luke touched her arms, still dancing. The music surged and returned and paused, surged even while pausing, paused and surged and pumped again. The only light was a strobe: Luke saw Nicole's arms and hair, coming and going, illuminated and vanishing, crackling into view and disappearing. Smoke began pouring onto the dance floor, so thick it was impossible to see. The trance deepened. The light became solid: purple, then green, then gold. Luke could not see, not even Nicole, not even his own arms. There was no distance or direction, only the impenetrable light, the endless pump of the music.

Their eyes were still as wide as planets when they left the club, just as it was beginning to get light. Being outside made them realize how out of it they still were. It felt less like the city was getting light, more like it was reconstituting itself, as if it hadn't been there in the night, as if it had dissolved and now, in the gray non-light, was becoming substantial again. As it did so they saw things they wouldn't otherwise have noticed: bits of buildings, architectural details whose names only Nicole knew. It became lighter as they walked. At boulevard Richard Lenoir the market stalls were being assembled. Vans were crowded with boxes of fresh produce. Scales were being set up, prices written on cards. The immensity of the effort of getting the produce here — sowing, planting, ploughing, growing, digging up and transporting — seemed out of all proportion to the end results which, when all was said and done, were only versions of the onions, carrots and potatoes they had eaten for dinner the night before. It didn't make sense.

'It would be nice if somewhere was open,' said Sahra.

'We could try the Kanterbrau,' said Luke. The sky was blue-gray now, birds were already flying in it. The Kanterbrau had just opened. They were the first customers. No one knew what to order, whether to opt for a nightcap or a morning coffee. Luke fancied a refreshing lager. Alex thought he'd have a refreshing lager too. Nicole wanted an orange pressée. Sahra was ready for coffee. Alex changed to coffee and so did Luke. Then he changed to an orange juice and the waiter trudged off, undaunted.

They were still full of chemically engendered expectation but that anticipation was gradually coming to refer to the past, to something that had already taken place. They were wide awake, distracted, glowing. They said things without being sure who had said them. Speaking and listening had become indistinct. Alex paid for the drinks. Their bodies were still full of the pump and color of the music so they went back to Luke and Nicole's and danced some more. When Alex and Sahra had gone home Nicole took a shower. She came back into the main room, wrapped in a towel.

'Do you want to watch or do?' she said.

AFTER A FEW HOURS' SLEEP the four were back together, still spaced out, tired and not tired, overcome by a lovely nostalgia for events that had taken place only hours earlier. Luke squeezed a jug of orange and carrot juice and then, as soon as they had drunk that, he made another jugful, this time adding a knuckle of ginger. Sahra lay with her head in Nicole's lap, drifting. Alex played records. They danced some more and reminded each other of things they had seen and felt the night before, in the club and in the film, the two parts of the evening becoming more and more deeply intermingled as they did so.

Alex and Sahra left, Nicole went to lie in the bath 'for two or three hours.' Luke tidied up and switched on the TV: rugby. With the sound turned down he forgot he was in France. He sat facing the screen, feeling suddenly alone, worn-out, dejected. The doorbell rang: Alex, back for something Sahra had left behind. As Luke opened the door to let him in he felt a surge of déjà vu. When Alex had retrieved Sahra's bag Luke returned to the TV, trying to locate the origin of that sensation, the original experience of which he had just felt the tantalizing echo.

He couldn't, of course, you never can, because although that misleadingly named sensation sends you scurrying into your past, the moment it urges you towards is *that* moment itself. And at that moment you glimpse the Eternal Recurrence as a potential fact, as a mechanism, rather than a metaphor. That is the solution contained in the riddle of déjà vu. All memories are premonitions, all premonitions are memories.

F OR HER PART, NICOLE WAS CONVERTED; after that weekend the four of them always took E when they went out dancing.

They also decided to spend Christmas together — without having any idea of what they would do or where they would go. Ideally they wanted to find a house in the country and spend the holiday there. Sahra had an uncle who, she thought, owned a house somewhere. She wrote to him the next day but heard nothing back. Staying in the city seemed a dismal option but, they agreed, if the worst came to the worst they would do that. They would cook a huge meal, get high and let the day ripple over them.

In the meantime, in various permutations, they went shopping for Christmas presents for each other. Sahra and Alex went looking for presents for Luke and Nicole; Nicole and Sahra went looking for gifts for Alex and Luke. Luke didn't go with anyone because he hated shopping.

'We've tried to do it a couple of times,' Nicole said to Sahra as they drifted round Magasin. 'But then, after about ten minutes, before we've even tried anything on, he starts moaning about how expensive everything is. We always end up just going for coffee or to a film. The only thing he likes doing is looking at records.'

'We go all the time,' said Sahra. 'I try on expensive cocktail dresses and Alex tries on expensive suits. Sometimes we even buy things. Not expensive things. Oh, let's go into lingerie.'

'Actually, that's one of the things Luke *does* like to buy. Or at least to look at.'

'Alex too.'

'We'll probably bump into them.'

The first displays were of nightgowns. Then girdles, substantial brassieres and large comfortable undergarments. As they walked further into lingerie, the items became progressively skimpier, more revealing, so that the shop seemed to be undressing itself. Then, gradually, lingerie gave way to shimmery evening wear.

'What now?' said Nicole.

'I'd like a coffee.'

'You're as bad as Luke! Actually I'd love a coffee too.'

They went to a café on rue Saint Honoré. The waiter brought their coffees and a handful of sugar cubes. The wrapping of each cube was illustrated with the flag of a different country. Nicole held them one by one and Sahra tried to guess which country was represented. First was a tricolor: a white stripe bordered by two greens.

'Nigeria,' said Sahra.

'Good,' said Nicole. She held up another tricolor: red, white and green, with a tiny emblem in the middle of the white.

'Mexico.'

'Very good,' said Nicole, picking up a red flag with a yellow star in the center.

'Vietnam.'

'You'll never get this one.' It was an absurdly crowded flag: four horizontal bands — blue, white, green, yellow — a red stripe running down the middle and a yellow star in the top left-hand corner.

'Central African Republic,' said Sahra without hesitation.

'How did you know that?'

'Alex and I were at a place with the same sugar last week. The same ones came up.'

'Cheat! What a coincidence though.'

'Not really. They're only the flags of coffee-producing countries.' Nicole threw the Central African Republic at Sahra. 'Alex wanted to get Luke to come to a place where they have the same sugar and bet on how many countries he could name,' said Sahra. 'He knew Luke wouldn't be able to resist it and he'd make a fortune out of him.'

'He would have, I'm sure.'

'I'm not sure I am in the mood for serious shopping today,' said Sahra.

'Me neither.'

'Shall we go to a film instead?'

'What would you like to see?'

'I don't know, we'll have to look in the paper.'

'It's a shame Luke's not here. He spends so much time checking the times of films in *Pariscope* that he knows them all by heart.'

'And Alex.'

'They're funny aren't they, these English men?'

'Nothing they say is serious.'

'And everything is.'

'Yes.'

'Still, at least they dress nicely.'

'Too bad they look like working at that warehouse for the rest of their days.'

'They love it there.'

'I know. But it's strange not to have *any* ambition, don't you think?'

'Luke is so lazy. He claims he came to Paris intending to write a book. I think he wrote about half a page. If that. And he has this idea of doing some stupid film about the 29 bus but he never will, I'm sure. He *has* learned some French but basically as long as he can play football, sleep with me, get stoned, go for drinks at the Petit Centre with Alex and go dancing at the weekend with the three of us he's perfectly happy.'

'Alex is the same.'

'At least he can speak French. And he's not *obsessed* by those things.'

'Only because he's got Luke to do his obsessing for him.'

'Actually, do you know what I think Luke is really obsessed by?'

'You?'

'No. Happiness. For most people it's incidental, almost a side effect. But all of Luke's energy — and that's why he's so unambitious in other ways — is focused on living out his ideal of happiness.'

'Then I *was* right,' laughed Sahra. 'You're the embodiment of that ideal.'

MC Solaar came on the radio or jukebox or whatever it was. The two women knew the song well and sang the first line together: '*Le vent souffle en Arizona. . . .*' Then they drank their coffees, tapping the table, listening.

> '*Il erre dans les plaines, fier, solitaire*
> *Son cheval est son partenaire*
> *Parfois, il rencontre des Indiens...*'

'*Alex* est son partenaire,' laughed Nicole.

'They're like that aren't they?'

'Et nous sommes les Indiens.'

'Actually, that's been a big breakthrough for Alex. *We're* partners. Which is a very new thing for him. A few weeks ago he came across something in Saint-Exupéry about how love means not looking *at* the person but looking in the same direction. He's taken to that like a religious conversion. I sometimes think we're more like friends than . . .'

Sahra paused because Nicole appeared distracted. She was thinking about Luke and, for the first time, was troubled by the way he looked at her, the way he was so obsessed by her beauty, by having the proof of his happiness before his eyes.

'I'm sorry,' said Nicole. 'I was thinking about something you said. Go on.'

'No, it was nothing. Nothing important.'

'Really?'

'Yes.'

'Do you ever think about the future?'

'Funny question. Why do you ask?'

'Because I never do.'

'I don't either. I think that's one of the things about taking E. It becomes impossible to think about the future. The present becomes all-consuming. Or at least the past extends back only as far as the weekend before.'

'And the future as far as the weekend to come.'

'Yes. It's actually a stupid drug, don't you think? You never have any thoughts at all when you're on it, let alone interesting ones.'

'That's probably why the boys like it so much.'

'No thought, only sensation.'

'It *is* bad for your head though, don't you think? It takes so long to get over it, and even when it's over it's not over. Two days later you mean to say one word and another comes out. You want to say chair and you say table.'

'You do that anyway, Nicole!'

'That was only in English. Now I'm doing it in French too.'

'Maybe we *should* think about the future,' said Sahra. 'Shall we try it now?'

'OK.'

'Ready?'

'Yes.'

'Go.' They shut their eyes and thought hard for several moments, holding hands as if at a badly attended seance.

'Well?' said Sahra.

'Nothing.'

'Me neither. Unless you count Christmas presents that we still haven't bought.'

'That's better than me. When I try to think about the future I always end up thinking of the past. As if they were the same thing, as if the future had already happened.'

'How do you mean?'

'Well, Luke and I slept together the first night we went out and I think that's why. Although I hardly knew him it was as if I already knew him, as if we already *had* slept together. It wasn't like he seduced me — I don't think he'd know how to seduce any-one — or I seduced him. It was the most unsurprising thing that has ever happened. In some ways I feel I've always known him.'

'I know what you mean,' said Sahra. 'I can't imagine you not being with each other. Maybe it's because I met you both at the same time.'

'I can't imagine not being with him either,' said Nicole. 'But I *can* imagine him not being with me — but I can't imagine him being with anyone else. Whereas although I can't imagine me not being with him, I can imagine me being with someone else. Does that make sense? I'm not sure I followed it myself.'

'The really difficult thing to imagine is Alex without Luke.'

'Or vice versa.'

'It's like: buy one and get the other free.'

'Luke says they're like brothers.'

'That's because he doesn't *have* any brothers,' said Sahra, more sharply than she'd intended, as Solaar came to the end of his rap:

> *'Toujours à contre-jour, c'est bien moins héroique*
> *Dans le monde du rêve on termine par un happy end*
> *Est-ce aussi le cas dans ce quel l'on nomme*
> *Le nouveau western . . .'*

CELESTIAL BATH

Yan Geling

THE CLOUDS BRUSHED over the sharp blades of grass. The shafts, heavy with seed, undulated, each wave bowing before the next.

Wen Xiu sat on the slope watching Lao Jin run downhill, becoming small as a prairie dog. Wen Xiu had been chosen by Lao Jin from among the Intellectual Youth to learn how to herd horses. The day she had followed Lao Jin to the herding site, she saw there was only one yurtlike, round military tent and realized she would have to share it with Lao Jin. Before she had come out, the Livestock Bureau had told Wen Xiu that there was no need for concern about Lao Jin: his thing had been lopped off long ago. Some decades before, there had been a blood feud out here. The opposing clan had grabbed Lao Jin, then eighteen years old, and run a knife between his legs. Since then he had been bereft of his manhood. There had already been six, maybe seven, girls among the Intellectual Youth who had learned how to herd horses with him, and none had ever come back carrying Lao Jin's foal. The feuding war party had definitely scraped him clean.

Nonetheless, Wen Xiu detested Lao Jin. If it weren't for Lao Jin's choosing her, she would still be together with several hundred other Intellectual Youth back at the powdered milk plant. One time she asked Lao Jin why it was he had selected her, of all people, to herd horses. Lao Jin replied, "You have a horse's face."

Wen Xiu was not considered ugly; back in middle school in Chengdu, she certainly wasn't. She was just a little short and skinny. Her body was like a wasp's, her waist only two hand clasps in circumference, making it look like she had two segments. When she mounted or dismounted a horse, Lao Jin would run up to her with both hands taut and outstretched and say, "Up we go!" or "Down we go!" He would hold her, supporting her buttocks with one hand and using the other to lift her by the underarm. Wen Xiu sensed that Lao Jin's hands really wanted to do something else. She hadn't been on the prairie for long before several men tried to feel her up, and it was usually done under the guise of teaching her how to mount or dismount a horse. Afterward, Wen Xiu herself would surreptitiously touch the parts that the men had touched, as if by doing so she could restore them. The Livestock Bureau put on outdoor movies. When the movie was over, as soon as the generator was shut off, ten or more Intellectual Youth girls would yelp, "Bastard! Damn your ancestors!" They had all been felt up. At that moment several dozen flashlights would intersect their beams, their shafts of light piercing the night sky like spears planted helter-skelter. That was just how the guys here got their jollies.

Since she had started herding with Lao Jin, she had not been to see a movie. In order to go, she would have had to sit behind Lao Jin on a horse, hanging on to his waist for twenty or thirty kilometers. The last thing Wen Xiu wanted to do was to hug Lao Jin's waist, and if that meant no movies, then so be it.

AROUND TEN KILOMETERS FROM THE TENT, at the foot of a slope, there was a shallow stream. The only way Lao Jin could collect water was by dragging a leather pouch flat along the stream's bottom. Yet any time that Wen Xiu complained of itchiness, Lao Jin would tell her there was a way to take a bath. She would hear him singing as he drew water and knew that he was singing for her ears only. Lao Jin was a first-rate singer. His singing had the music on the loudspeakers of the Livestock Bureau beat hands down! Sometimes his song sounded like a horse whinnying, other times like a sheep laughing. When she heard it, Wen Xiu felt like tumbling down the grassy slope, even though Lao Jin seemed to be singing about his troubled heart and his inexpressible dreams.

Lao Jin was singing his way back from the stream. His singing came closer. As he climbed up the grassy slope, she could already smell the horse scent on his body.

He smiled at her. His beard was withered, and his chin was barren. Sometimes, when he was idle, he would fumble with the remnants, seeking out dead bristle, then rooting it out.

She looked at him with one eye shut to avoid the bright sunlight. "Hey, Lao Jin! Why'd you stop singing?"

"Got work to do."

"But you sing so well!" It was the truth. There were times when she hated him. Hated herding horses with him. Hated sharing a tent with him. At times she wished Lao Jin would just die — but not the song. The song should follow her, even when she left this place.

"Gotta stop singing," Lao Jin said, smiling bashfully.

Wen Xiu hated his gold front tooth, which ruined a perfectly good smile. If it weren't for that, he would not have looked nearly so fierce and frightening.

Lao Jin's full name was Jin something-something, four syllables long. If you were walking behind a band of Tibetans and called out that name, at least ten of them would turn around in response. Wen Xiu didn't bother to remember the name. Lao Jin, Lao Jin — much easier for everybody. Lao Jin was forty-something years old, but he looked older than that. Tibetans don't keep track of their birthdays, so you couldn't be sure if he was still in his thirties or had already reached fifty. Unlike other old herdsmen in the Livestock Bureau, Lao Jin had not accumulated any personal property. He owned neither a wristwatch nor a fountain pen. His most valuable possession was his gold tooth, and even this he had inherited from his mother. She had told Lao Jin to knock it out as soon as she died, so the man who performed the sky burial couldn't take it. He later had the knifesmith inlay his own tooth with the gold. The knifesmith knew how to inlay any bone-handled knife, and he used the same technique to inlay Lao Jin's tooth.

THE WATER-FILLED LEATHER SADDLEBAGS DANGLED on both sides of the horse's rump. Lao Jin lightly whipped the horse's round buttocks with his palm, and the horse hauled the water up the slope. The horse's belly, stuffed pendulously round from grazing, crooked off to the left, then to the right. Lao Jin followed its gait, his stocky muscular shoulders dipping and angling down this way, then that.

If you didn't know his story, you couldn't tell that Lao Jin lacked anything that other men had. Especially when Lao Jin lassoed a horse. His whole body formed one unbroken arc with the rope, taut as a bowstring. Once the horse straightened its legs to run, Lao Jin had him. In these prairies there wasn't another man for hundreds of miles around who had such a deft and powerful hand.

Lao Jin poured the two big leather saddlebags full of water into the oblong ditch he had dug at the summit of the slope. The ditch was rather shallow. A little deeper and one could just fit a coffin in it. The ditch was lined with a sheet of black plastic from a torn-up bag of horse fodder.

Wen Xiu sat downhill from the ditch, her body facing down the slope, her head turned back toward Lao Jin. After watching him for a while, she asked, "What are you doing?"

"You'll see," Lao Jin replied.

He peeled off his shirt. It had been soaked with sweat and dried by the sun, so it was pasted to his back like a medicinal compress. When it came off, it made a "ssslah!" sound, and a puff of vapor blew out. As he poured out the contents of the saddlebags, the water in the little pool rose. It was over half full.

Wen Xiu's neck was sore from turning her head back to look. "What are you up to now?" she persisted.

"Just wait and see," Lao Jin replied in a low growl. Every time Wen Xiu got on or off a horse and didn't want Lao Jin to help her, his lips would part over the gold tooth while he growled like that. The sound contained a womanly pique completely inconsistent with Lao Jin's massive trunk and wide prairie face. There was also a sort of beastlike affection in it.

Wen Xiu stared blankly down the slope toward the horses. Lao Jin took a seat on the ground not far from her, pulled out a tobacco pouch, rubbed the tobacco leaves on his thigh and rolled himself a fat, thick cheroot. Then he stuck it in his mouth and began lighting it all the way around. Wen Xiu heard the crude matches skittering, heard them breaking, and looked at Lao Jin as he fumbled with his makeshift cheroot, giving him a narrow-eyed smirk of "serves you right." Only after ten or so matches had been broken or extinguished in the wind did he succeed in lighting the cheroot, which protruded sideways out his mouth like some kind of artillery cannon. Under the bright noonday sun you couldn't see the lit end of the cheroot and you couldn't see the smoke, just stringlike shadows swirling about Lao Jin's face. The smoke stank: as the cheroot burned shorter, the stench grew worse.

Smoke was also rising off the little pool. Inside its vapor the transparent air warped and shimmered. The sunlight was absorbed by the black plastic, heating the water. And all in less time than it took Lao Jin to enjoy his cheroot.

Curious, Wen Xiu walked up the slope toward the pool at the summit. She tested the water with her hand and cried out, "It's scalding hot!"

"You can bathe in it now," Lao Jin replied.

"How about you?"

"Go ahead, you bathe. Pretty soon it will be too hot to bear."

She knew Lao Jin didn't bathe. The first time he had held Wen Xiu dismounting from a horse, she realized that this was a man who had never taken a bath in his life.

"I'm going to take my clothes off now," Wen Xiu said.

"Go ahead," Lao Jin replied, continuing to stare.

Wen Xiu pointed down the slope toward the herd. "You go round up the horses. Some of them look like they're about to stampede."

Lao Jin, a little put out, slowly turned his head away from her. "I'm not going to watch you."

Wen Xiu squatted on the ground. "But I can't bathe with you here!"

Lao Jin didn't move. He knew she wouldn't pass up the chance to bathe. She loved bathing. The first night she'd ladled out a basin of water and put it at the foot of her straw bedroll and blown out the lamp. Just as she had stripped off her panties, she heard the rustling sound of Lao Jin's straw bedroll stirring.

As she had squatted, straddling the basin of water, carefully dipping the towel in the water so as not to make a sound, Lao Jin had become deathly quiet. She felt as if Lao Jin's ear hairs were standing on end.

"Bathing?" Lao Jin had finally said in an intimate tone.

She had paid no attention to him but splashed temperamentally with her hands, making the water sound like a flock of ducks landing on a pond.

Lao Jin had then taken the initiative to break the embarrassing silence, saying, "Heh, heh! You Chengdu girls just can't get along without bathing."

It was from that time that her hatred for Lao Jin had begun. The next day she had slapped together a canvas partition to wall off the corner with her cot and bedroll from the rest of the tent. By now, Wen Xiu was almost completely undressed. "You mustn't turn your head," she warned.

Lao Jin had his back toward Wen Xiu. He raised his head to look at the sky and remarked, "The clouds are coming this way."

Wen Xiu, now completely naked, said, "You're not allowed to turn your head!"

Then she stepped into the pool. First she let the hot water roll over her and hissed with relief as she soaked in it. It made her feel so good that she gave out a silly giggle. She knelt in the pool and used the hand-sized washcloth to scoop up water onto her body.

Lao Jin sat rigidly immobile without turning his head. The place where he sat was lower down on the slope. If he turned his head, he could not see Wen Xiu completely. Wen Xiu, however, kept staring vigilantly at the back of his neck while she rubbed her body with scented soap. Before she picked up the soap, she first shook her hand dry. If her hands were too wet, it would waste soap. That's what her mother had taught her. Wen Xiu's father was a tailor and knew how to save customers' cloth. In all the years her parents had been married, Wen Xiu's mother had never had to buy her own cloth.

"Lao Jin, sing another song!" Wen Xiu requested, now finished with washing and enjoying a good soak.

"The clouds are moving this way." Lao Jin shifted his gaze from one end of the sky to the other, as if watching the clouds move, then deliberately turned his head toward where Wen Xiu was. He saw her flour-white shoulders with a dark-burnt face perched on top. The whiteness of her body in the pool appeared a blur, like moonlight stroked and ruffled on troubled waters.

Wen Xiu cried out shrilly, "Damn you, Lao Jin!" and she splashed soapy water at him.

Lao Jin quickly turned his face back around, sat down again properly and wiped the water off his face with his green cotton Mao cap.

"May your eyes rot out!" Wen Xiu cursed.

"I didn't see anything," Lao Jin protested, still wiping water off the tip of his nose and lips.

"If you did see anything, may your eyes rot out!"

"I saw nothing."

AFTER A WHILE WEN XIU WAS READY TO GET DRESSED again. At the bottom of the slope two men came by, each astride a yak. They were driving a herd of yaks to the slaughterhouse. Both of them were quite familiar with Lao Jin and called out, "Lao Jin! Lao Jin! What are you doing squatting up there?"

"Don't come up!" Lao Jin growled back.

"What are you doing? Squatting to take a piss, huh?" Having said this, the man at the front yanked the reins of the yak he was riding and circled around the back of the slope, heading for the summit.

"Don't come up!" Lao Jin quickly turned his head toward Wen Xiu and barked, "Get dressed."

By now the men had discovered Wen Xiu cowering there, covering up her body, but they still pretended they had come up to give Lao Jin a hard time. "Lao Jin, everyone says you've got to squat like a woman to take a piss. Today we caught you in the act. We want to watch!"

Lao Jin dragged his rifle off the ground and looked through the sights, carefully sizing up the two of them. When the pair tried to proceed forward, the rifle sounded. One of the yaks reared up into the air, then turned its head and careened down the slope diagonally, its body in profile. It was now shorn of one horn and had lost all sense of balance and direction.

The man who had been bucked off the yak called, "How dare you shoot at us, Lao Jin, you son of a bitch!"

Lao Jin dribbled some spittle onto the rifle barrel and wiped off the gunpowder stain with the corner of his jacket. He made no sound and showed no expression, but just acted as if nothing had happened. Then he loaded another bullet into the rifle's belly and said to the other man, who was still sitting dumbfounded on his yak not knowing whether to advance or retreat, "You want one, too?"

The man hastily pulled the yak's head around. From its back he yelled, "Just you wait, Lao Jin, you son of a bitch!"

"Wait for what? For you to come and bite my balls? I ain't even got my tool no more!" Lao Jin yelled. With both hands he slapped his crotch, whacking it powerfully, pounding a fair amount of dust out of his trousers.

Wen Xiu burst out laughing. She felt Lao Jin's fearlessness was genuine: without that thing to determine his fate, no one could threaten his life.

*B*Y A CERTAIN EVENING IN OCTOBER, Wen Xiu had been herding horses with Lao Jin for exactly half a year. That is to say, she had graduated. She could now lead a platoon of Intellectual Youth girls in herding horses. In the morning she woke up early, stuck her head out from behind her canvas partition and asked Lao Jin, "Do you think they'll come today to take me back to the Livestock Bureau?"

Lao Jin had just entered the tent, cradling in the crook of his arm a load of firewood wrapped in a layer of white frost. "Huh?" he replied.

"It's been six months already. They said after six months I could return to the Livestock Bureau. It's been one hundred and eighty days. I've counted them."

Lao Jin relaxed his grip, and the firewood came rolling out onto the ground. He was wearing a military fur coat with his own alterations. Both the sleeves had been removed, exposing his long apelike arms from the shoulder, which gave him the appearance of being both dexterous and clumsy. He was looking at Wen Xiu.

"You're leaving?"

"Leaving?" she replied. "It's my *turn* to leave." She gaily tilted her sharp little chin as she drew her head back behind the canvas curtain.

She started laying out clothes, deciding what to wear. From two identical old outfits she pulled out one, held it up to the light and looked at how many tiny holes had been shot through it by sparks from the fire pit. No, that wouldn't do. She looked at the other outfit, but it wasn't much better. With a sigh, she finally put it on. With a gauze scarf and her hair combed nicely, she wouldn't look too messy. When she stepped out of her enclosure, Lao Jin had already brought the butter tea to a noisy boil.

Making conversation, Wen Xiu asked, "Have you eaten yet?"

"Cooking," Lao Jin replied, pointing to the fire.

Seeing her nicely dressed and made up, his eyes followed her, his hands mechanically snapping off twigs. Then she took a piece of mirror broken in a triangular shape and handed it to him.

Immediately he stood up and held it for her. She didn't need to say a word. He would raise and lower it according to her unspoken wishes.

WEN XIU SPENT A WEEK IN THIS MANNER, arranging her gauze scarf and braiding her hair. The person who should have come from the Livestock Bureau to take her back had not come. On the eighth day, Lao Jin said, "We've got to break camp and move on from here. The heavy rains have changed the course of the stream. There won't be any water for the horses to drink, and there won't be any for us either."

Immediately Wen Xiu started to protest loudly. "*Move* again? Move *again*? When the Livestock Bureau sends someone for me, we'll be even harder to find." She glared at Lao Jin, her small round eyes quivering out two accusatory teardrops — the Livestock Bureau must've all died off, seven days without seeing hide or hair of them, and all of this is your fault, Lao Jin!

As the days passed, Lao Jin did not bring up the matter of moving camp any more. Every day he took the horses farther afield to find grass that was not too parched. Wen Xiu no longer herded horses with him. She spent each day waiting at the entrance of the tent.

One day someone arrived. It was a peddler with an ox cart selling goods to all the various herding camps. He asked Wen Xiu if he could come in for some buttered tea. As they sat on the floor and talked, he told Wen Xiu that over the past half year, the Intellectual Youth had begun to be withdrawn from the herding camps and were returning to the city. The first to go were those whose families had clout. Next were those with good connections at the Livestock Bureau. Almost all the girls among the Intellectual Youth had gone: they had all established a "good connection" to the Livestock Bureau.

When Wen Xiu heard this, she stood there with her mouth gaping.

"Why haven't *you* left?" the peddler asked, as if prying at some shameful secret of hers.

"They've all gone, and I'll go, too . . . when I feel like it . . . go back to Chengdu." Both the peddler's knees pressed against Wen Xiu's knees.

Wen Xiu stared at him blankly. The peddler was apparently a former soldier. He had a pair of eyes that had seen it all. All the good jobs out here went to ex-soldiers.

"For a girl like you," the peddler said, "getting good connections at the Livestock Bureau should be no problem at all!" He laughed and spoke no more. Then his lips went to Wen Xiu's face, neck, between her breasts. . . .

THE PEDDLER LAY ON TOP OF WEN XIU groping and rolling, crushing the straw in the bedroll. Wen Xiu wanted to go back to Chengdu. Mom and Dad couldn't help her. She could only rely on herself to find a way out. The peddler was the first way out that she found.

As the day was approaching evening and Lao Jin walked back into the tent, he heard the rustling of straw behind Wen Xiu's canvas curtain. Under the curtain, Lao Jin could see a pair of men's cloth shoes tossed on the ground, soles facing upward. Lao Jin didn't realize that he had been standing in the tent, immobile, for over an hour, until it was pitch black both inside and outside the tent.

The peddler came out from behind the canvas partition wearing the cloth shoes, the backs crushed flat. He didn't see Lao Jin. The peddler went straight to the opening of the tent, lit up by the rising moon. The ox harnessed to the cart woke from its slumber as the peddler climbed in. He turned on a transistor radio and rode off, singing as he went.

From Wen Xiu's bed came not a hint of human sound. She

was still alive; she just lay there as if dead, turning her eyeballs back and forth awkwardly in the darkness. "Lao Jin? Lao Jin, is that you?"

"Uhn," Lao Jin grunted in reply, shuffling his footsteps around to signify that everything was normal.

"Lao Jin, is there any water?"

Lao Jin brought over a cup of butter tea. Wen Xiu's head popped out from under the canvas curtain. Just then, the moonlight shone on it, and Lao Jin saw that her head and face were soaked with sweat, wet like a newborn lamb. She drew her mouth closer to drink. Lao Jin leaned forward and supported her head. She frowned slightly, as if to extricate herself from the palm of Lao Jin's hand.

"No water, huh?" she said in an accusatory tone.

"Uhn," Lao Jin grunted once more and dashed out of the tent. He dragged over his riding horse. Swinging his leg over its back, he gave it a vicious kick with his heels.

Lao Jin rode the ten kilometers to the little brook at the foot of the hill, the one where he had drawn water for Wen Xiu to bathe in that day under the hot sun. He took two military canteens and filled them until they could hold no more. By the time he got back the moon was already high in the sky. Wen Xiu was still inside her canvas enclosure in the corner of the tent.

"Come have a drink! Water's here!" Lao Jin called out, almost gaily.

He passed a canteen through to Wen Xiu. Very soon he heard an "oo-too! oo-too! oo-too!" sound as she poured it into the metal basin. After a while, Wen Xiu stuck her hand out again, beckoning for the second canteen.

"I brought it for you to drink," Lao Jin protested.

Saying nothing, she just snatched the strap of the canteen and dragged it inside her canvas enclosure. Once again he heard the sound of water. She was bathing again. She just couldn't get along without bathing, Lao Jin thought, especially today. After a while, she threw some clothes on and walked out, carrying the basin of water with both hands. She walked out of the tent and went a considerable distance before she finally threw out the water.

To Lao Jin, the way she walked was no longer very becoming.

"Lao Jin," she said, handing him one of the canteens deferentially, "there's still a little water left. Would you like a drink?"

"You drink it," Lao Jin replied.

Insisting no more, she took an apple out of her pocket and carefully aimed the spout of the canteen at it. The water came out in a thin stream. She turned the apple evenly with her other hand, washing it on all sides. She raised her eyes and saw that Lao Jin was looking at her. She smiled briefly and then began, "ka-chaw, ka-chaw!" to gnaw on the apple. The peddler had given it to her. She held it with both hands while she gnawed on it. There was really no need to use both hands, however: it was quite small.

WEN XIU CONTINUED TO STAY in the tent all day while Lao Jin went out to herd horses. Every night when Lao Jin returned, he would see a big pair of men's shoes under the canvas curtain. One time a shoe had been tossed a couple of meters outside the curtain, almost to the edge of the fire pit in the middle of the tent. Lao Jin picked up the fire tongs in one hand. He looked at the shoe as it lay there, sizing it up. Then he grasped the shoe with the fire tongs and dropped it into the fire. The shoe's leather roasted until it sizzled and small beads of oil began to seep out. Then it started to twist and puff out cloying clouds of smoke which gradually turned to ashen white. Its stench filled the whole tent.

Lao Jin recognized this shoe. Few people in the grass-lands could afford to strut about in a shoe like this. There was one in the Communist Party Committee of the Livestock Bureau, two in the Livestock Bureau's Personnel Department. Only these three.

A FEW DAYS BEFORE, WEN XIU HAD TOLD LAO JIN, "These people coming to see me are important people, you know."

"How important?" Lao Jin had asked.

"Extremely important. They all have the power to approve documents. To go back to Chengdu, without some important people to approve some documents and stamp their seals on it, there is no way out." She looked at Lao Jin, but it was hard to say where her gaze was focused. Her tone of voice was a low mono-tone, just like Lao Jin's when he was bored and frustrated and went outside to pour out his heart quietly to his horses.

For his part, Lao Jin looked at her with a dazed expression, like an animal that understands emotions but doesn't understand human language. She hadn't been out herding for some days now, and a layer of skin on her face, scorched by the intense sun, had started to peel off. Through the cracks of the burnt surface, pinkish tender flesh had begun to appear. While she was talking, her nails would fly quickly over the skin on her face, scraping lightly. Her sharp fine nails gradually picked open a fissure; then a spot of new flesh about the size of a wild broadbean flower began to emerge.

"I'm too late — all the other Intellectual Youth girls did this years ago to get the Livestock Bureau to send them home. By now they've probably all found jobs in Chengdu. Think of it, a girl with no money and no connections, isn't this the only asset she's got left?" As she spoke, she lifted up her eyes, as if to express her justification. She also told him it wouldn't work if she slept with one without sleeping with the others. Those you didn't sleep with would block your way.

*L*AO JIN NODDED HIS HEAD as he rolled a stronger than usual cheroot on his thigh. Wen Xiu had told him everything. She didn't tell him because she particularly cared about his opinion. Just the opposite — it was because he couldn't possibly have an opinion. After all, what kind of opinions could livestock have?

The canvas curtain rustled for a bit. The man was looking for his second shoe. He kept groaning "son of a bitch." Lao Jin sat with his spine turned toward the curtain, smoking his cheroot, puffing vigorously, flattening out his lungs.

The man was in a tight spot. He couldn't allow Lao Jin to see him under the kerosene lamp and make a one hundred percent positive identification. He was much too important a person in the Livestock Bureau for that, and terribly busy. When he had arrived, he hadn't even bothered to exchange a polite greeting with Wen Xiu; he just went straight to what he had come for. Since her lamp had been dark the whole time, he didn't have any idea what Wen Xiu looked like.

The man's predicament caused Wen Xiu to confront Lao Jin. "Lao Jin, did you see a leather shoe anywhere?"

"Whose shoe?" Lao Jin answered.

"What do you care? Did you see it?" Wen Xiu said, raising her voice. She walked over to stand directly in front of him. Her hair hung disheveled on both sides of her face. Her body was enveloped in a green military overcoat, revealing a slice of breast at the top, a shaft of thigh at the bottom. The light from the fire pit danced on her face, which had become so thin that it looked hollow, and her sunken eye sockets looked like a pair of caves.

"I *asked* you a *question*!" she said even louder, both pleading and demanding.

Lao Jin only paid attention to his smoking, inhaling until his chest cavity was taut, then flattening it out like a bellows.

"What are you, a yak? Don't you understand people-talk. . .?" Wen Xiu huffed as she squatted down on the ground in front of him, the bottom of the overcoat parting, revealing both that which may be exposed and that which may not be. It was as if in front of livestock there was nothing to be ashamed of, as if human modesty were superfluous.

Lao Jin heard the important person slip out behind his back, half-shod.

Wen Xiu was still wrapped in her overcoat, pacing back and forth bare-legged through the tent. She picked up a canteen and rattled it. Empty. The other one, also empty. They had been camped out on this bone-dry stretch for over a month now. Every day Lao Jin had had to ride the ten kilometers to fetch two canteens of water. From that day on, her water supply was cut off.

F OR FIVE DAYS THERE WAS NO WATER. To drink, there was only milk and buttered tea. No longer did just one man a day come to see Wen Xiu; sometimes there were two, even three. At night, no sooner would Lao Jin hear one leave than the next would come in practically on his heels. The path to the door of the tent had been trodden smooth. Lao Jin hung a piece of dry thornbush in the doorway, hoping to scratch somebody's eyes out with it. But they all stealthily tiptoed around it. Now the most important precaution they took before climbing into Wen Xiu's bed was carefully to hide their shoes.

At dawn of the fifth day Wen Xiu was practically at her wits' end. She hadn't slept all night and couldn't figure out who the men were that she had been with. After the very last one had left, she finally crawled out of bed. Lao Jin watched from his own bed as she dragged her footsteps over toward his bedroll and declared to him, "Lao Jin, for days there hasn't been a single drop of water!"

Lao Jin looked into her two wild eyes and saw that they were bloodshot. He also got wind of a not-to-be-reasoned-with type of odor emanating from her body. With the loss of her water supply, she seemed to have lost her last shred of dignity and rationality.

Lao Jin slowly, in a stately manner, started putting on his clothes, muttering as he dressed. His pants, spotted with sweat stains and permeated with dust, had become so stiff that they almost stood up by themselves at his bedside. He pulled them over and began to put them on, though it wasn't clear whether he was wearing them or they were wearing him.

Wen Xiu walked over to the extinguished fire pit, her eyes scrutinizing the strip of twisted and burnt shoe sole, not registering what it was. She yelled at Lao Jin at the top of her voice, "What the hell are you doing, dressing so slow?"

Lao Jin immediately stopped his movements.

Wen Xiu, sensing something less than wonderful on its way, mouthed an even worse rebuke and glared at him.

Lao Jin walked up to her. "You're prostituting yourself, don't you know?"

Wen Xiu was still glaring at him. Then she gave him a sidelong glance and a coquettish little sneer. "What did you say?"

"You're a whore," he said.

"Not for you," she answered.

BY LI DONG, THE BEGINNING OF WINTER, Wen Xiu lay in the infirmary. She had just had an abortion. Her bare legs lay on a two-inch-thick sheet of grainy brown blotting paper to absorb the flow of blood. Lao Jin kept a vigil outside her room, waiting for someone to call him in. But no one ever did. The nurses all openly referred to Wen Xiu as "Worn-Out Shoe" and "the wild nymphet." It was just like that Intellectual Youth boy in the surgery ward whom people openly referred to as "Zhang Three-Toes." Supposedly his rifle had misfired and shot off three of his toes. After his wounds had healed, Zhang Three-Toes was headed back to Chengdu. He was trading all his possessions for caterpillar grass. Once he got to Chengdu, it would fetch a good price at any reputable herbal medicine shop, and besides, it was light to carry. Everybody knew that he had purposefully taken aim at his foot and sheared off his toes, crippling himself. Once he could no longer ride a horse, all they could do was send him back to Chengdu.

On the third day of Lao Jin's vigil for Wen Xiu, Zhang Three-Toes walked by and sat next to him on the same bench. He gave Lao Jin a cigarette, then entered Wen Xiu's hospital room.

It was only after he had smoked the cigarette halfway down that Lao Jin felt something was wrong. Suddenly he stood up and pushed on the door of the room. It was locked from the inside. Lao Jin extended his legs and took a stance, then sent his bronze-tipped boots flying and flashing against the door. His roars of "You animal! You beast!" caused the whole shift of nurses to come running. Soon all the beds in the ward were empty as well. Even the paraplegic patients rolled their wheelchairs down the hall to gawk at the commotion at Wen Xiu's door.

Several nurses restrained Lao Jin from kicking the door, but he kept yelling "Beast! Beast!" His cries grew progressively hoarser.

Zhang Three-Toes walked out of Wen Xiu's door, and everyone cleared a path for him. He tossed back his greasy head of hair with the devil-may-care attitude of a proud hoodlum. Addressing the crowd, he said, "What are you doing? What's the fuss? If you want in, get in line!" He pointed at Wen Xiu's door, then pointed at Lao Jin. "Lao Jin's first in line, I'll vouch for that!"

Lao Jin lifted up one of his bronze-tipped boots and stamped it down on Zhang Three-Toes's remaining toes. Zhang Three-Toes neighed like a horse.

The nurses yelled at the crowd to disperse. Then they had a loud discussion among themselves.

"It wouldn't matter to her if it were a stud donkey!"

"The bleeding just stopped and already she's luring guys into her bed."

Lao Jin returned to his place on the wooden bench.

IN THE MIDDLE OF THE NIGHT, A BLIZZARD STARTED. Lao Jin was awakened by the cold. He saw that Wen Xiu's door was open, but her bed was empty. He waited awhile; she did not return. Lao Jin went outside to search for her, shivering with panic. He found her at the side of the road, fallen to the ground. The snow had coated her hair white. She said she had gone out to get some water. She really missed water; she wanted to take a nice, refreshing bath.

Lao Jin picked her up and embraced her, her body flush against his own. Her face was swollen to the point of transparency, but it was still pretty. Her little wasplike body was pitifully small, shivering and trembling inside the palms of Lao Jin's enormous hands. Lao Jin held Wen Xiu for a while, standing in the blizzard. He did not take her back to the infirmary. He carried her toward the stables where his horse was kept. Each time the wind came up, he would turn his spine toward it, walking backward. Wen Xiu drifted in and out of consciousness. At one point, she felt something warm dropping on her face, and she was astonished. She never thought that he might be able to cry, or that he would shed tears for her.

THE NEXT DAY THE SKY HAD CLEARED. The grass on the prairie was covered in mournful white. The scrub was bereft of its leaves; on its tightly interlaced twigs hung bright crystalline icicles.

Lao Jin was sitting under a scrub tree, watching Wen Xiu a short distance away fumbling with the rifle. She had already told him that today was the day she wanted to carry out her plan. She had learned something from Zhang Three-Toes. Lao Jin's cheroot dangled from his mouth, long since extinguished. He waited for the rifle to sound.

The shadow of Wen Xiu's ravaged body was delicate and small, and one of her braids had come undone. For some reason, she turned her head to look at him.

He said nothing and showed no expression; the extinguished cannonlike cheroot between his lips made no motion.

She smiled at him briefly. Then she placed the rifle on the ground.

"I'm afraid I won't aim right," she said. "It's hard to shoot yourself. I just can't bear to do it." Her voice was quavering.

She smiled again and put the mouth of the rifle on her foot, raised her chin and closed her eyes, like a child not daring to face its pain. "That's better. Hey, just as soon as I fall over, you'll take me right to the clinic, won't you?"

"I will," Lao Jin replied.

"I'm going to shoot now — hey, you'll tell them that I was carrying my rifle and it accidentally went off, won't you?"

"Of course I will," Lao Jin replied again.

Her face was white as snow, her lips chewed blue. The rifle still did not sound. She spoke to Lao Jin again. "Lao Jin, turn your head away. Don't look at me."

Lao Jin pulled his green Mao cap straight down to his chin, confining his face inside it. For a while, outside his hat, it was eerily quiet. He lifted his hat to take a look and saw her on the snowy ground, rolled up into a little ball, the rifle lying on the ground one pace away.

Her face full of tears, she said to Lao Jin, "Lao Jin, I beg you, please help me. I just can't bear to shoot myself. . ."

Lao Jin looked at her.

"Lao Jin, I'm begging you, if you get one good shot off, I can go back to Chengdu. Winter's coming. There's nothing I hate more than the winters here! None of them would help me. You help me, please! You're the only one who can help me now . . .!" Suddenly she rushed over, hugged Lao Jin tightly and pressed her mouth against his lips, dry and acrid with years of accumulated tobacco smoke.

Lao Jin extricated himself from her embrace and went to pick up the rifle. She gazed at him like one who is rescued, with a look of complete trust.

Lao Jin held the rifle across his body and retreated a few paces. Then he retreated a few more.

Wen Xiu stood up straight, looking directly toward the rifle barrel.

Suddenly, she asked Lao Jin to wait. She carefully plaited the braid which had come undone. Her eyes kept looking at Lao Jin. She smiled again wanly.

Instantly he understood. From her poise and her unperturbed manner, he understood the detachment, the transcendence of a farewell. He suddenly knew what she wanted him to do.

Lao Jin set the rifle to his shoulder. Gradually he raised the rifle barrel higher. She remained motionless, as if about to have her picture taken.

The rifle sounded. Wen Xiu swooned and fluttered to the ground, her mouth emitting the groan of a woman at her moment of peak satisfaction. Lao Jin put down the rifle; he knew there would be no need for a second shot.

WHEN THE SUN HAD REACHED the middle of the sky, Lao Jin placed Wen Xiu's pure, pure white body into the shallow rectangular pool. It had been filled with snowy slush which Lao Jin had now heated to the temperature that had always made her feel most comfortable.

Her eyes were closed, and in the vapor her body looked like the image of an Immortal on a temple fresco.

Lao Jin now removed his own clothes. He studied carefully his own body's incompleteness, then looked at the peaceful Wen Xiu. He turned the rifle barrel around, aiming it at his own breast. One end of a rope was tied to the trigger, the other end to a stone. Then he kicked the stone, and as the stone rolled down the slope, a shot rang out, and hot blood gushed out of his chest.

Lao Jin crawled toward Wen Xiu and submerged himself in the pool. He held Wen Xiu. In a little while, the snow would cover them both completely.

Translated from the Chinese by Lawrence A. Walker

The Good Outside

Shaun Levin

NOW THAT ALL THE OTHERS have said their goodbyes and gone home for the night, Peter and Davide sit alone in the garden. Eventually they'll begin to talk about Jonathan. Davide will start, Peter will be reluctant. He'd rather sit quietly for a while and then head off to bed, to the sofa in fact. He hasn't slept much since leaving Italy, and it's been a densely hot day outside in the garden. But now, with everyone gone until tomorrow, the air seems fresher. Twilight takes the edge off the lingering heat.

Cushions and mattresses are scattered across the lawn, and there's a low coffee table under the apple tree. Someone brought it out for those sitting in the shade by the fish pond. This was Jonathan's garden. He had tomatoes and zucchini along the one wall, gooseberries along the back wall and flowers along the third wall and around the small patio where Davide and Peter are sitting. Their table is covered with most of the mugs, glasses and plates people had used during the day. Everything needed to be cleared away and tidied before people came back in the morning.

The second day of the *shiva* had been long and drawn-out. Peter had spent most of the day, like the day before, gathering up as much news as he could. He'd been in Italy for ten years. He'd left South Africa as soon as he thought of himself as a painter, and being an abstract artist he believed he carried his inspiration inside him. He'd left South Africa to get away, really. And from what? From death and from politics. At first he'd had a lover, Gianni, and then it was just himself in the small house he'd bought with his mother's money.

Davide was Jonathan's boyfriend. Peter the painter watched him from the moment he arrived at their house, hoping to catch memories of Jonathan in Davide's gestures. He watched him greet people with a pained smile that showed gratitude, like in-laws accepting gifts for a bride and groom. He watched Davide cry and saw him being comforted by friends and by Jonathan's mother. It was only when Davide was quiet, alone, physically present but his mind elsewhere, when he sat like that on one of the cast iron chairs, legs folded, elbows on the armrests, that Peter saw Jonathan. Davide the writer and Jonathan the surgeon were there together.

DAVIDE HAD CAUGHT PETER STARING at him during the day. He could tell Peter knew he was keeping something from him. He felt pity for Peter, and saw how he longed to be told that he meant a lot to Jonathan. But Davide wasn't going to lie. He didn't have to; Peter wasn't his friend. He watched Peter trying to get people to talk to him. He noticed how he listened. Jonathan had told him that if anything Peter was a good listener. But then someone would come up to Davide and embrace him, and sit by his side for a while, and then go off to join one of the groups in the garden.

The larger group, mainly friends of Jonathan's, had spent the day at the edge of the garden under the apple tree. Peter sat with them most of the time. They'd all been to school together. Every so often a shriek or muffled giggle came from the group, and if Davide turned to look, someone would point up into the tree by way of an explanation and an apology. Another group had stayed nearer the round table on the patio, near Davide, close to the food.

Peter and Davide sit at that table in silence, each slowly moving away from being part of a gardenful of people to being alone together, something that hadn't happened very often over the past, what was it, twelve years? As far as Peter remembers he's never been alone with Davide, Jonathan's boyfriend. He wants to say: You two built a lovely home here. But Davide speaks first.

"Our Jonathan," he says.

Peter imagines Davide is about to tell him that Jonathan left him something of great significance.

"What a fucking slut he was," Davide says, throwing his head back and laughing out loud.

"Slut?" Peter says, telling himself not to smile.

"All day I've felt secrets raising their heads. Like rats."

"What secrets?" Peter says.

"Was it just me," Davide says, "or did he keep secrets from everyone?"

"Not from me he didn't," Peter says. "He never kept secrets from me."

P ETER HAD KNOWN JONATHAN since nursery school, since they were little boys at the Summerstrand Hebrew Nursery School. Since they were two bricks and a pisspot high. They'd go snake hunting in the veld behind the Greek grocery shop and comb the dunes near Peter's house for bits of broken clay to piece together. They went to the same junior school, and in high school Peter was head boy and Jonathan deputy head. They were a good team. It was like being kids, playing sheriff against the baddies. They told each other everything.

"So you knew all about this, did you?" Davide says.

"About what?" Peter says.

"All these strange little affairs he was having," Davide says.

There was that period of five years when they went off to university: Jonathan to become a doctor, Peter to study art. They'd written lively, graphic letters to each other and spent three of the five summers together in PE. The other two summers they traveled abroad: Jonathan to Europe, Peter to his mother's family in Israel.

"It must have been during those trips that the secrets began," Davide says.

"What kind of secrets?" Peter says. "He told me everything. He always told me everything when he got back."

"So you did know, then?" Davide says.

Peter could have given examples, and he was tempted to. But Jonathan had made him swear never to tell anyone. Not about the sex he'd had with the two eighty-year-old men in Paris. He got chatting to a beautiful Moroccan in a café near the Eiffel Tower who sold sex to men in old-age homes. They were so old, he told Peter, they smelt like his grandfather. Their arseholes were as loose as saloon doors. And not about the arrest on the other trip, this time to London, where he'd been caught in the public toilets on Leicester Square sucking someone's cock.

Dead Jonathan had told Peter all this and more in elaborate detail. They'd be lying on his bed, his bags still unpacked, the duty-free bottle of whiskey almost empty, laughing and kicking their legs in the air like upturned cockroaches. Jonathan went to fetch more ice from the kitchen and on his way back stood over the bed and said: Don't you dare tell anyone about this. Ever. And Peter said: I swear. Cross my heart. And when, some years later they'd laughed again about these incidents, just before Peter went off to Italy, Davide already in the picture, Jonathan made Peter swear never to tell a soul.

"I don't know anything you don't know," Peter says.

"Then why are you so silent?" Davide says.

"Am I?"

That wasn't all Peter knew about Jonathan. He knew about the bad patch. Jonathan had found out about Davide's affair and played on his Catholic guilt. Davide believed adultery was a sin, and that hell was a real place. And in all their years together, Jonathan had never told Davide about his infidelities. He used Davide's one slip to keep the accusing finger pointed away from himself. Jonathan wrote to Peter in Italy about cruising on Donkin Hill and landing up in strangers' beds. Just two years ago there'd been that black guy, the ANC guy, who'd taken Jonathan to his room in the church where his mother worked. Jonathan said they were thinking about coming to Europe.

"I hate not knowing," Davide says. "I hate that he's dead and left me with all these stories I have to find out."

"Shouldn't we go inside?" Peter says. "Let's take all this stuff into the kitchen."

IN ALL THE TWELVE YEARS Davide had been Jonathan's boyfriend, he hadn't heard him utter a good word about Peter. Davide had been dreading this evening. He hadn't expected Peter to come to the funeral. Then he'd hoped Peter would be delayed in Italy, or that he'd have an exhibition he couldn't get away from. He'd met Peter a few times before he left South Africa. But he'd heard Jonathan's stories. Peter would take Jonathan drinking and Jonathan would drink more that he'd intended. He'd land up sharing things with Peter he'd meant to keep to himself. But no one knew him like Peter did and there was no one else to confide in. He told Davide, proudly at first, and then as if he was burdened by it, that his relationship with Peter had no room for small talk.

"It was all so heavy," Jonathan had said. "Heavy and abstract. Even with all the alcohol."

Davide and Jonathan were relieved when Peter finally left. Jonathan would write Peter the occasional letter, and Davide looked forward to Jonathan confiding in him. He was, after all, a writer, and writers knew how to listen, too.

"There couldn't have been any big secrets, could there?" Davide says. "I mean, how many secrets can a man have? You'd think that after twelve years I'd know all of them."

"The in-between secrets are the tricky ones," says Peter. "The little indiscretions people think they've already shared with lovers, but somehow forgot to mention. The tiny things that slip people's minds because they're there all the time. It's like you don't tell your lover about the mole on your back. He knows it's there."

"He loved telling me secrets," Davide says.

"He did love telling secrets," Peter says.

They are discussing him in the past tense. So soon. Too soon. Fighting over him like vultures. Tearing him apart as if that would keep him alive. Like Bacchus.

"What a day," Peter says.

"And there's more tomorrow," Davide says.

Davide had insisted the *shiva* be held at their house. And because it was summer, almost Christmas, and they had no air-conditioning, they'd had the *shiva* in the small, clean, well-kept garden. Things hadn't gone smoothly. Jonathan's father had walked out that morning.

"Solly wasn't happy," says Peter.

"'I will not have this turned into a garden party,'" Davide says, sitting upright in his chair, hands on his hips. "'This whole thing looks like something out of Alice in fucking Wonderland to me.'"

"Jonathan would have loved that," says Peter.

Solly's wife, Mina, had tried to persuade him to stay, but he wouldn't listen. She followed him through the house to the front door. She stopped there and watched him march down the road to get the car. She'd have stayed if he hadn't driven up to the front door and said: Are you coming? She turned to Davide who was standing behind her in the kitchen, embarrassed, putting cheese and crackers onto a tray.

"I hope they come back tomorrow," Davide says.

"Maybe you should give them a ring," Peter says. "I still remember their number off by heart."

"All the numbers have changed since you left," Davide says.

THE SKY IS STRIPS OF PURPLE and navy blue and dark pink clouds. Peter notices how deep the colors are in the garden. Oranges and purples and whites, bold against the chrysanthemum leaves. The sweet-pea blossoms were beginning to turn brown, and the tomatoes were too ripe, the zucchini too heavy. Jonathan had planned to pick and cook them the weekend they took him to the hospital to die.

"Everything's changed since I left," Peter says. "Nothing's the same."

"We've got democracy now," Davide says. "We're the happy rainbow nation."

Peter's hungry and wants Davide to offer him food. The mourners had all brought their offerings, as was customary, and there were at least two untouched dishes in the kitchen. One of them was Jonathan's Aunt Gertie's famous cheese sticks.

"Part of you gets taken away when they die," Peter says. "A big part."

"I think I'll give all his clothes to charity," Davide says.

"What?" Peter says.

"I don't want to see friends wearing his clothes."

Davide was sitting in his chair like Jonathan. He looked like a writer, surveying the garden, detached, just like Jonathan did when he was in doctor mode. Peter, too, had adopted a way of being, a way of sitting that suited the reclusive artist he had become. Three posers, he thought, which made him think of the photograph of him, Jonathan and the third gay man in their class at school.

"Simon hasn't been here yet," Peter says.

Simon was a fashion designer with a chain of stores across the country.

"I wish he'd come," Davide says. "He'd know what to do with the clothes."

"He did call earlier," Peter says. "He'll be round tomorrow."

"No one told me he called," Davide says.

PETER WAS STARVING and couldn't take his mind off the large silver plate of cheese sticks arranged neatly around a bowl of avocado dip. He'd dip them into the creamy spread and eat them with the bread-and-butter pickles Mina had brought. It was when she turned up with the large preserving jar that morning that her husband, Solly, had said: I will not have this thing turned into a garden party.

Hunger pangs last for twenty minutes. In less than twenty minutes he'd be fine. He'd have lost his appetite. From where he's sitting that seems unlikely. He knows exactly what those cheese things with the avocado dip are going to taste and feel like in his mouth. And those pickles. He remembers them from when they were kids. Just two bricks and a pisspot high, Mina used to say.

"His shirts," Peter hears Davide say. "I think I'll give his shirts to Simon. He did make most of them."

Peter hadn't seen Simon since moving to Italy. He didn't know Jonathan had kept in touch. Maybe there were secrets. About five years ago, when Jonathan came to visit him in Italy, soon after Gianni moved out, he told him about the Saturday mornings him and Barry Sher would go oyster hunting in the rock pools in Summerstrand and sell them for twenty cents a dozen to the Marine Hotel. Peter couldn't remember. And even though thirty years had passed, he still felt left out and jealous that he hadn't even known about something he could've been part of. There must have been other things.

"What kinds of secrets?" Peter asks Davide.

"Oh I don't know," Davide says. "Nothing comes to mind. But just from sitting here in the garden, hearing people talk about him, I know there were things I didn't know."

"Maybe they're just that," Peter says. "Things you didn't know. Not necessarily secrets."

"Maybe," Davide says.

HOW AWKWARD JONATHAN WOULD HAVE FELT seeing Peter and David together in his small garden, chatting away. The three of them, as far as Peter could remember, had hardly ever been alone together. Except when he'd had boyfriends before he left for Italy, and Davide and Jonathan would invite him, and the boyfriend, for dinner.

"Remember Steve?" Peter says. "He called this morning from Jo'berg."

"You should have let me speak to him."

"Why him?"

"He was your ex," Davide says. "That makes him part of the family."

"Hardly," Peter says.

"I liked Steve," Davide says. "He was a nice guy."

"He was a shit," says Peter. "He went back to his stupid wife."

"But he left her again," Davide says. "Maybe he'll come tomorrow."

The garden will be filled with people tomorrow. Peter will have old friends to gather more news from. There'll be Simon to fill him in, and Mina to remind him of when he was a boy. He needs all this to take with him back to Italy.

"Do you want something to eat?" Peter says.

"Maybe just a little something," Davide says. "I'm not that hungry."

"What would you like?" Peter says.

"Maybe some of those cheese things," Davide says.

"I've been thinking about them," Peter says.

"I tasted one when she brought them," Davide says. "They're perfect."

"I'll bring the whole plate then."

Peter is glad to be alone in the house. The lights are off, so he makes his way through the house from memory. He leans against the kitchen doorway. He'd helped Jonathan take the door down when he moved in. He could still see where the hinges had been screwed off, the holes covered up with Polyfilla and painted. Even after Davide had moved in, and was asleep upstairs, they'd come back to Jonathan's kitchen at the end of a night out. Now Peter walks in and bumps his hip against the butcher's block that hadn't been there when Jonathan moved in.

"They're over there," Davide says.

"What's that?"

"I hid them," Davide says. "The cheese sticks. I hid them behind the microwave."

Peter takes the plate of cheese sticks and dip and gets serviettes from the drawer by the sink.

"Still in the same drawer," he says.

"You know what's frustrating?" Davide says, opening the fridge and taking out a bottle of wine. "I can hate him all I fucking well like and it won't make a difference."

"Yes," Peter says.

"Solly won't talk to me about Jonathan," Davide says. "He won't tell me a thing. Mina does. But I want the stories from him. He's punishing me. He's keeping the stories to himself. You tell me about Jonathan."

"I haven't heard from Jonathan in ages. You must know that," Peter says. "I had one letter from him in the last two years. All he did was write to let me know he had the virus. He never answered any of my letters after that. Why did he stop writing?"

"This is horrible. This is not the way it should be," says Davide. "We're like two fucking building blocks in some kid's game. Pull one block away and look what happens."

"Why did he stop writing?" Peter says.

"I don't know, Peter," Davide says, gripping the wine bottle in both hands. "I really don't know. I just don't want to feel so empty."

Peter puts down the plate and serviettes and opens his arms for Davide. Davide frowns at him.

"Please don't make me cry," he says.

Peter takes the wine bottle from Davide and puts it on the counter. He holds him and Davide cries into his shoulder. Peter's body turns to stone and, eyes wide open, he looks over Davide's shoulder. He stares blankly through to the garden where the man who will love him is standing. He is waiting for Peter to come to him, having seen how bravely he holds this man's grief. And then Peter will be comforted.

Davide smells of sweat and two-day old aftershave. He isn't going to shave or wash during the *shiva*, and that morning he and Jonathan's mother had covered the mirrors with scarves and pillow cases. Davide's body trembles and Peter feels his flesh moving against him. Davide feels so empty he wants to cry.

At Rome airport five years ago, when Peter had driven Jonathan there to catch the plane back to South Africa, Jonathan had hugged him in the waiting lounge. Peter had cried like a little boy being abandoned in the world. Jonathan had held Peter's cheeks in his palms and for the first time ever kissed him on his lips. Then he got on the plane and Peter went back to his little house, back to speaking Italian to everyone, back to finding ways to translate his demons into shapes and colors. That's all he had to rely on. Now he is grateful for Davide's fingers pressing into his back.

Davide is a stranger in a foreign country. He feels himself getting smaller and smaller. This isn't his home anymore. From the moment Peter walked in it stopped being his house. Was this how he used to feel when Peter spent the night? Is this why he made sure he was asleep before they came back from their drunken binges? As if knowing Jonathan longer made the house more Peter's than his. Peter carries images of Jonathan from a time when Davide did not know him, so he digs his fists into Peter's back and opens him like stage curtains.

"What am I supposed to do?" Davide says.

Davide loosens his grip from Peter's back, and Peter is alone again.

"Let's eat," Peter says, stepping back and offering Davide a cheese stick.

"And drink," Davide says, taking up the bottle of wine.

Back in the garden Davide makes space on the table for the wine and the glasses and the plate of cheese sticks. Then he pours wine into the glasses, and they wish each other long lives, as is custom. V

I hear my train a comin.
—JIMI HENDRIX

BREAD AND THE LAND

Jeffery Renard Allen

BLACK FLUTTER, MAMMA FLASHED ABOUT THE ROOM, work-bound, her shiny knee-length black leather boots working against the wood floor like powerful pistons. Up, down, up, down. She stopped and visually searched the space around her. I have everything, she said. The hem ends of her long black dress flared like wings.

Yes you do, Hatch said. He waited patiently on the bed edge, warm, his snowsuit packing him tight in heat and sweat.

She put herself before a full-length mirror, flexed a black hat onto her plump head and slipped inside a black fur coat. The hat was real fur, but the coat some imitation material.

You look dashing, he said.

Thank you.

He watched her with hot pride. She was heavyset but pretty. Even with her second chin, she was ten times prettier than the mother of any classmate at school.

The phone rang from the faded brass nightstand next to the bed. Uh. Who could that be? People always call you at the wrong time. She lifted the receiver to her ear. Hello. Her eyes widened. It's Blunt, she said.

Oh, he said. My grandmother. He didn't like his grandmother. You must go to work, he said. Tell her. Be frank.

Words chirped in the earpiece. Mamma brightened. The preacher's dead, she said.

Oh, he said.

The preacher's dead.

That's good, he said.

She gave him a hard look. Placed her hand over the mouth-piece. Don't get smart.

He didn't say anything.

Put those things in Mamma's bag, she said.

A small duffle bag lay unopened on the bed.

Okay, he said. He picked up her rubber gloves, pulled the fingers and let them snap.

She looked at him. You know not to make noise when I'm on the phone.

Fine. He crammed the gloves, a white smock, white rubber-soled shoes, deodorant and a bar of soap into the bag, which spread at the sides, stuffed like a holiday turkey.

Yes, Blunt, Mamma said. Okay, Blunt. I understand.

Blunt and the preacher lived in New York City, in Harlem, point of origin for a nationwide chain of funeral homes. Just around the corner, a Progressive Funeral Home entombed an entire street, the name spelled out in orange square blocks lit from inside, like supermarket letters. A man-high wrought-iron fence surrounded and secured the parking lot, four red brick columns for corners, each topped with a white globe at the end of a long, stem-slim black metal pole.

Blunt and the preacher own that, Mamma liked to say.

Yes. Blunt. My grandmother.

Snooping, he had found two other Progressive Funeral Homes listed in the telephone directory.

Name and deed, Blunt traveled through his mind like some inky shapeless substance. He had never spied a photograph — Mamma had burned all existing images many years before he was born — nor heard her voice. Once a month Mamma mailed Blunt a letter with his most recent portrait, and Blunt mailed her a letter — typed, always typed — with a check.

Why doesn't Blunt send us more money?

She sends all she can.

How much is that?

Whatever she sends.

Fine.

Goodbye, Blunt, Mamma said. She hung up the phone. Turned to Hatch. Smiled. Hatch, come here.

What? he said.

Come over here to Mamma.

Is this something frank?

Yes.

What?

Blunt's coming to live with us.

Nawl.

Don't use that street language.

I'm not.

Choose your words carefully.

Who's coming to live with us?

Blunt.

My grandmother?

Yes.

Why is she coming to live with us?

Because the preacher's dead.

So?

The preacher's dead, so now she can come live with us.

How come she didn't come live with us when the preacher was alive?

You know why.

No I don't.

Don't talk back. And don't talk countrified.

How come she never visited us?

You know why.

I don't know why. Tell me. Be frank. Good people are always frank.

I am being frank.

You ain't.

Watch your language and stop talking back.

I ain't talkin back.

Mind your mouth.

How did the preacher die?

Suddenly.

Oh.

You know that the preacher had a bad heart.

Who had a bad heart?

Be a good boy for Mamma.

I am being good.

Then we'll let Blunt stay in your room when she comes.

Nawl. I don't want her around me. He liked his small room, high above the world, a third-story nest where he flew for refuge.

We're going to move your things into my room so that Blunt can put her things in your room.

Nawl.

It'll only be for a little while. Blunt has lots of money now and

she wants to buy us a house and we'll all live together and you'll
have a big room.

She lyin.

Watch your mouth. You get worse every day.

I do not.

And stop talking back.

He said nothing.

You can sleep in my room when she comes.

Nawl. I'll sleep in the kitchen *if* she comes.

What did I tell you about talking back?

I'm not talking back.

She *is* coming.

Fine.

Okay?

Fine.

You'll be a good boy for Mamma when she comes?

Fine.

She knows how smart you are.

Fine.

THE TRAIN SCREECHED AROUND THE CURVE, the
passengers firm and erect in their seats like eggs in a car-
ton. Hatch checked flight conditions. The El was a strong, sprawling nest erected over the city. Safe, Mamma beside him, he looked
down on the world far below. Wormlike people wiggled through
snow. Habit, they often rode like this, all day on Sunday. Mamma
wanted him to memorize every route. He would touch the map
like his skin.

Car to car, the train pulled into the station, a flock of magnet-
ic, migratory birds. They quit the bright metal insides and, hand
in hand, pushed through the rushing crowd. His snow-suited legs
rubbed together and made a noise like an emery board against fin-

gernails. He kept his eyes low, sighting varied shoes and boots flopping like fish across the wet concrete floor, his blind forehead colliding with belted or fitted waists. His sight lifted to bright lights perched pigeonlike in the high conical roof.

Some fabled creature waited near the checkpoint to Gate 12. Human, beast and fowl. Feathery white mink hat and coat, red amphibian jumpsuit (leather? plastic?) and knee-length alligator boots. She was tall and wide like a man and carried a white suitcase in one hand, a black guitar case in the other.

Mamma swallowed. That's Blunt, she said.

The creature called Blunt spotted Mamma, and strode forward without hesitation, strode, full of life. She halted two feet shy of them and set down the suitcase and the guitarcase with equal care. Extended her hand. It was big. Mamma took the big hand into her own.

Hello, Joy, Blunt said.

Hello, Blunt, Mamma said.

Blunt released Mamma's hand. Seemed to think twice about it and gave Mamma a quick peck on the cheek. Studied Hatch. So this is my little Hatch, she said.

He watched her back. She was butt ugly. A net of wrinkles drew her skin tight. Her dark face masklike, coated with rouge. A flat pug nose some fist had mashed in. And long protruding jaws and lips, like a stork's mouth. Nothing baby about her face. Nothing. Thinking this, he was forced to admit that she had pretty eyes. Green.

Come give your granny a hug, she said. Spread her arms wide. He didn't move. She bent down and hugged tight, forcing his constricted lungs to breathe in her perfume. Strawberry pop. He didn't like strawberry pop.

She released him and rose back to her full height.

Where's your other suitcases? he asked. Mamma pinched him.

She only pinched; she would never strike him. She'd had two still-births; he was her only child.

What? Blunt asked.

Where's your other suitcases? Mamma pinched him again. If you're coming to live with us then where's your other suitcases? You can't put nothing in no one suitcase.

Blunt gave him a fierce cold look, eyelashes so stiff with mascara they resembled tiny claws. Now, you're a smart little boy so you know I'm having the rest of my things shipped.

I don't know nothing.

Mamma looked at him, hard.

Blunt green-watched him. Such a pity. You look so cute in that snowsuit.

THEY LEFT THE STATION FOR THE TAXI STAND. A storm had set in; snow sprayed his face, white wet and cold. Blunt walked over to the lead cab, a fat yellow block, and roused the driver, a short man with short thick legs.

How you today, ma'am?

Just fine, Blunt said.

The driver placed her suitcase inside the yellow trunk.

She opened the passenger door, slid the guitarcase on the floor, then held the door wide. Mamma motioned for Hatch to get in. He did. She followed. Blunt held her hat with one hand, ducked inside the cab and seated herself. Mamma hadn't held her own hat. Blunt shut the door. The motor roared into life. The driver slammed the taxi into gear. Where to?

Mamma told him.

Enjoy your ride.

They rode to the dull hum of the busy engine, the heat full blast, Hatch damp, his body boiling beneath the snowsuit. He studied Blunt's reflection in the driver's rearview mirror. She sat very stiff, green eyes staring straight ahead. Glad that he didn't have to sit next to her. Glad that Mamma occupied that middle space between.

Easy motion and casual heat, they cruised in bubbled metal. No one moved. No one spoke. Forgetting each other in the silence. Three monkeys, deaf, mute and blind. They rode on past Hatch's school (Andrew Carnegie Elementary). Mamma gestured to Blunt. Blunt nodded and smiled. Then traffic started to thicken. The driver took cautionary measure, dodging around the El's pylons, only to get pinned between a pylon and some stalled cars.

Move this thing sir, Blunt said.

I'm doing all I can, ma'am.

Well move it.

I'm sure we'll be moving soon, Blunt, Mamma said.

Look, I'm paying you good money! Blunt watched the driver with her green eyes.

This will go much better if we all jus relax, the driver said.

Hatch peered through the frosted window. Thickly clothed people hurried by with their heads tucked against slanting wind and snow. Sheltered inside a doorway, a musician vied for attention. He was seated on a footstool, acoustic guitar angled across his body, strumming the strings and tapping an athletic-shoed foot, an empty soup can a few feet in front of him. His voice rose above snarling traffic and honking horns.

> *If you don't wanna get down wit me*
> *You can't sit under my apple tree*
> *Say, if you don't wanna get —*

One passerby tossed him a coin. Hatch felt all twisted inside. He caught Blunt's face in the rearview mirror. She too was watching the musician, effort in her looking. All the anger seemed to have left her. She saw Hatch seeing her and gave him an icy look.

She faced the driver. Driver get this cab moving, she said.

He did, foot on the accelerator to race down lost time. The Progressive Funeral Home soon blinked by. Against Hatch's expectations, both Mamma and Blunt sat oblivious. He grunted. That Blunt! She ain't look at it cause she don't want me to know she ain't nothin but a phony.

They braked to a quick stop, bodies thrown forward and back. Blunt pulled rolled bills from a jumpsuit pocket, unfolded them and licked her thumb and forefinger to catch the crispy edges. She paid the driver and tipped him five dollars. You don't deserve a tip, she said.

He smiled. Thanks anyway, ma'am. I'm gon get yo suitcase from the trunk.

Mamma frowned at his vocabulary.

Only if you're capable, Blunt said.

He's using that countrified language, Hatch said. The driver shot Hatch a glance. Mamma pinched him. But he speakin street. Mamma pinched him again. Stung, Hatch's arm was hot and hurt in the snowsuit. Hand on the doorhandle, he tried to make a quick exit. The door refused to budge. Frozen perhaps. Blunt leaned across Mamma and opened it. She smiled. Hatch gave her a mean look.

They quit the cab, snow crunching underfoot. The short driver hoisted the suitcase from the trunk, while Blunt pulled the guitar-case from the floor.

All y'all have a nice day, the driver said. He shot Hatch another glance and grinned.

Mamma shook her head at the diction. Hatch gave the driver his meanest look.

Blunt passed the driver another five dollar bill. Learn how to drive, she said.

Yes ma'am. Thank you. He got inside the cab and speeded off.

Three flight of stairs spiraled a challenge to the apartment above. Mamma started up, Blunt following — the suitcase in one hand, the guitarcase in the other — and Hatch following her. At the top landing Mamma leaned her tired weight on the banister, sucking for air. Seem like the *fourth* floor, she said. Blunt said nothing. Unfazed. Chest rising slow and easy. Hatch believed himself an excellent judge of age and had concluded that Blunt was *very* old — she was so ugly — but having witnessed her feat on the stairs, he was now uncertain.

YOU GOT A NICE APARTMENT, JOY. She looked the kitchen over with her green eyes.

Thank you, Blunt. It's small, but comfortable.

Well, don't you worry about that.

Mamma smiled.

Would you like some breakfast?

I sure would. Where do you keep your pans?

No. You must be tired from your trip. She lowered her eyes. Do you eat meat?

Blunt looked Mamma full in the face. Yes, Joy.

Well, let me show you to your room.

My room, Hatch thought. He was shaking with cold, his arm still hot from the pinch.

Mamma looked at him. Go into the bathroom and get out of that snowsuit. She and Blunt started for Hatch's room. He watched them.

Joy, let Hatch keep me company. Blunt stopped her body like a truck and waited for a response.

Mamma didn't say anything for a moment. She turned and looked at Hatch. Hatch, hurry out of that snowsuit and come keep Blunt company.

Hatch watched Blunt, hard. Wind and snow had smeared the makeup around her eyes, the talon streaks of some huge bird.

Mamma came forward and gripped his hand. Be good, she whispered. Don't be mean and selfish like your father. She had been frank about his father. Normally these words about his bad father would have settled him. He struggled to free his hand.

Be good, Mamma said.

He knew she would not hit him. No matter how angry she became. Mind working, he stared through the distance at Blunt. Formed a plan. He would pretend he liked Blunt. Alone with her, he would give her a piece of his mind. Choice words. All right, he said.

He freed himself from the snowsuit and hurried back. Mamma gave him a hard look that said, Be good. She pushed open one of the French doors which separated her room from his, then headed for the kitchen.

Hello, Hatch, Blunt said.

Hello, Blunt.

Blunt removed her coat and hung it in the closet. Her arms were thick inside the sleeves of the red jumpsuit. Then she was intent upon her reflection in the dresser mirror as she carefully removed her cap. Hair spilled gray and long about her shoulders. With her back to him, she began unpacking the one suitcase now open on the bed. She turned and smiled. Hummed low deep waters in her throat. You can't fool me, he thought. He watched her unpack and searched for the correct way to phrase what he wanted to say.

I MEAN, ALL THAT HAPPENED TWENTY-FIVE, thirty years ago. Blunt chased him out of town with her straight razor. Red they called him, though I never saw him myself. Clay-colored. Bow-legged. A midget. A bad man. Like your father.

Blunt kept his ten dollar Sears Roebuck guitar and taught herself how to play it.

Then Blunt married the preacher-mortician. I was ten by this time. They'd known each other all along. We moved into his funeral home. It was like a castle, enough rooms to sleep fifty people. Plenty places to wander and get lost.

The preacher always spoke his mind. Children make me nervous. This is what he said. I got a bad heart, and people like me with bad hearts also have bad nerves, if you see my meaning. I did. So I kept fifteen feet away from him. Fifteen feet. Measured it.

He was the most disliked colored man in the country. He kept a stable full of horses he had never learned to ride. (His bad heart.) And he had dainty ways like white folks. Always wore a suit and tie in the blazing heat, and walked with his head up high and breathed like a rusty well pump, and sweated like a fountain. He would place his napkin in his lap when he ate and sweat down into it. He had been in a car accident that scarred up his face pretty bad. (You should have seen it. Unbelievable.) And he never ate meat since it aggravated his scars. This is what he said: God saw to it to give me the accident and with it scars and a bad heart.

The accident had given him the calling to be a preacher but his sermons put people to sleep. (Christ is fire and water insurance!) That was what led him into the mortuary business. Preachers must eat. He was the picture of success. (They often wrote him up in the newspapers.) With the dead in your corner, you can't fail. Not that he didn't have his problems. Rumor had it that he disrespected bodies placed in his care. (I never saw him myself.) He carved tick-tack-toe on skin. He stuffed hollow cavities with marbles. He drained insides with a garden hose. He embalmed with shoe polish. These accusations turned away no customers. He was cheap and allowed payment by installments and gave a free vase of flowers and guaranteed his caskets to resist rust and rot for fifty years.

This man — his name always escapes me — took things one

step further. I was sixteen. One Sunday he entered the chapel shouting and screaming and cursing and woke the snoring congregation. He voiced his charges. The preacher had removed his wife's neck and put a short log in its place. And the preacher had wrapped that log in a pretty pink scarf to hide the evil deed. (I did see the scarf.) He pointed a sharp finger at the preacher. Your tail is mine, he said. And I got something for that hefty woman of yours too.

The preacher's nerves took over after that. He would not let Blunt leave the house. And when he went out into the street, he took me along with him as his eyes and his ears. He would look in every direction at once, scars twitching. Then he would put one hand over his heart desperate to calm it. But the hand would jump every few seconds like given an electrical jolt. Then the wheezing would start, and I would guide him back to the parlor. This went on for about a week, then he and Blunt grabbed their hats and coats in the middle of the night, and caught the first thing smoking.

I HEARD WHAT YOU DID, HATCH SAID. I know what you did. Mamma had always told him to respect adults, to speak when spoken to, but Blunt deserved no respect.

She stopped what she was doing, and turned to him with her green eyes and wild mascara. Her big shoulders tense and her big hand stiff. What did you hear?

You know.

You tell me.

No, you tell me. Why did you do it? Why? Speak up. Be frank.

She studied him for a moment. Sometimes it just bees that way.

Fine, he said. Neither understanding nor caring to understand, he went into the kitchen where Mamma was.

Were you good? she asked.

Yes.

Then why are you frowning?

I don't know.

You'll have to try harder to be good.

Fine.

Okay.

Fine.

A BURLY FOREIGNER UNDER AN UGLY RED HAT explains to a primly dressed man behind a desk why he wants a Liberty Express card. In our country it is forbidden to wear fur hats or ride speedboats. The white man issues him the card. He zooms off-screen in a long red speedboat. The camera zooms in on the ugly red hat buoyant on the water. Bubbles carry it under.

How many times had he seen that commercial over the day's slow course? They had sat in continual silence, no catching up on lost time, no planning for the found future. Mute monkeys.

Joy, why don't I prepare dinner.

No, don't trouble yourself. I'll do it.

Why don't we both do it. Blunt smiled.

You don't have to.

It'll be fun. We'll do it together.

I would like that, Mamma said. But why don't I cook and you stay here with Hatch and let Hatch keep you company.

Blunt hesitated. That's a good idea.

Mamma went in the kitchen. Blunt and Hatch watched the television.

Quiet day, Blunt said.

Yes.

Shadow and light, her face flickered. What's you favorite show?

The Phony from Harlem.

THEY SAT AROUND the round wood kitchen table with platters of fried chicken, black-eyed peas, cornbread and candied yams in easy reach. They sat like quiet spectators as if waiting for the food to perform. A roach crawled onto the table.

Mamma forced a chuckle. These roaches are about to run us out of here, she said.

Blunt smashed the roach with her hand, swift as a judge's gavel. Mamma turned her eyes away. Stunned like the roach, Hatch watched Blunt until she rose to wash her nasty hand. Mamma cleared the table. All three moved to the living room before the TV and sat down not saying anything. Blunt faced Hatch, some half-formed song in her wide throat.

He watched her. When you gon to play that guitar? he asked. Blunt was a phony and he would prove it.

Hatch! Mamma said.

Joy, it's okay. She looked at Hatch. Why don't you bring it to me.

Disbelieving, he rushed over to the guitar — invisible inside its armored case — tensed, stooped down and lifted it. It was light, weightless. He brought it over and set it down at Blunt's feet. Blunt shifted forward in her seat, crouched over the case, flipped open the latches and removed the guitar. Clean bright color. Sun and flame. And thick, cablelike strings which hovered an inch above the fingerboard and the sound hole (a deep dark cave). I bet that's Red's old guitar, Hatch thought. Too cheap to buy a new one.

Blunt plucked the strings with her right thumb — big as a shoehorn — while she twisted the tuning pegs with her left fingers, releasing long scraping vibrations like a dragging muffler. Hands working, she tested the strings some more, and nodded to herself when she achieved the desired pitch.

And now, for my next tune —

Hatch did not laugh at her joke.

She cleared her throat. Stroked the strings and set them humming. Opened her mouth wide in song.

> *Sweet daddy, bring back yo sweet jelly roll*
> *Sweet daddy, bring back yo sweet jelly roll*
> *Don't leave me this way*
> *Burdened with this heavy load*

Hatch's heart tightened. Music rode deep waves of thought and feeling. Carried him to some far off place in the room, where he sat alone, in a small boat, spiraling on a whirlpool of blue water.

Mamma started briskly for the kitchen. Hatch went dizzily after her. Mamma? Where you going?

To do my cleaning.

Come and hear Blunt.

I can hear her from in here.

Come hear. A lasting spray of blue water, cool on his skin.

Come see Blunt play.

You go back and watch her.

He went back. Why you stop? Go on. Play some more.

No. It's late in the evening. Folks trying to sleep. Blunt put the guitar back inside the case and closed lid and latches. Maybe I'll teach *you* how to play tomorrow.

Really?

Yes.

I'd like that.

Mamma came into the room. Hatch, bedtime.

Fine.

Time for bed.

Fine.

Goodnight, Mamma said. She kissed him.

Goodnight.

Goodnight, Blunt said. She kissed him, her big lips wet on his face, her pug nose hard against his cheek.

Goodnight. Anger dragged him from the room and to a dark, thinking place under Mamma's bedsheets.

He lay there for some time, weighing, calculating, then quietly left the bed at the precise moment Mamma and Blunt would falsely believe him asleep. He tiptoed over to the French doors and put his ear to the cold, squared glass.

Please try.

I will.

You know plenty. So please...

I understand.

Yes. That's all I'm asking. He's still young.

I will.

Well, I said my peace. Goodnight, Blunt.

Goodnight, Joy.... Daughter.

Hatch hurried back into bed and pulled the covers over his head. He heard Mamma enter the room. Felt the opposite side of the mattress sag under her weight. He kept his back towards her as a wall and waited for sleep to come.

I MUST LEAVE FOR WORK.

Why? Blunt said. I see no need.

Mamma seemed to ponder the words. Thank you, Blunt. I'm glad to hear you say that.

No need to thank me. Those bones is tired. It's time for some rest.

I won't argue.... Well, I better get Hatch to school.

You two go ahead. I'll stay here and get some rest. Still ain't got that train out of my system.

Okay, Mamma said.

Goodbye, Blunt, Hatch said. He smiled up at her.

Goodbye, Hatch. Yall need money for a cab? It's a bad day out there.

That would be nice, Mamma said.

RUBBER BOOTS INCHES ABOVE THE FLOOR, Hatch floated on the seat, an astronaut in his inflated snowsuit.

Why did I have to go to school today?

Because that's your responsibility.

You got frank with me about Blunt and the preacher and you got frank with me about my father because you want me to be responsible? She had once explained it to him.

Yes.

Is Blunt responsible?

Why do you ask?

She still be responsible if she run away from the preacher?

Good people stick by those who are good to them.

The preacher was good?

Yes.

That's not what you said.

What did I say?

You know what you said.

You misunderstood.

He was good?

Yes.

Why?

He helped her.

Are you being frank?

Yes.

They curved to the curb.

Be good. She kissed his cheek.

I will. He wasn't sure if she had been frank.

She paid the driver. Driver, could you please wait? I'll be right back.

You said it.

They quit the cab and took the short path to the school.

Be good.

I will.

WHEN SCHOOL LET OUT, he found Mamma waiting for him in an idling cab. He spoke excitedly about a typical school day. They had a quick easy ride home, the cab seemingly sliding above the snow like a great yellow sled.

Blunt! Blunt! We're home!

He ran freely through the apartment. Blunt's eyes stopped him, heavy on mind and skin, holding him in place like paperweights.

What happened to your eyes? Hatch asked. They're blue.

I'll show you. Blunt moved into Hatch's bedroom, her large body in blue silk pajamas, hair flowing like a silver wave down to her nape. She returned with a small plastic case resting on her palm. These are contact lenses, she said.

What? Hatch said.

She removed something from the case, raised her hand to her eye. Removed her hand. Now her eye was green. The other was still blue.

How'd you do that?

Contact lenses, she said. She held out the case, full of many colored lenses, painted Easter eggs.

Wow.

Those are lovely, Mamma said.

Blunt smiled with radiant satisfaction. Eager to please, she turned her eye gray, then light brown, then green, then blue again.

LAHZONYAH, BLUNT CALLED IT. LAH-ZON-YAH. He tried to rise to his feet, but found himself anchored to the seat, his stomach heavy with sunken treasure. The long, empty casserole dish abandoned in the middle of the table like a beached boat.

Play some music.

Mamma glared at him over the hot coffee at her lips.

Maybe later, Hatch. Let my food digest first.

How long will that take?

Blunt laughed. Do you know that I used to have my own place where I could play music anytime I wanted and where dozens and dozens of people would come to see me?

Mamma noisily returned her cup to the saucer.

What did you call it? Hatch asked.

The Red Rooster.

Did it look like a red rooster?

Blunt laughed. No. Like a barn. The only barn in Harlem.

Did it have —

Saturday, we should do some sightseeing, Mamma said. The coffee steamed up into her face. You haven't seen the city.

That'll be fine, Blunt said. How does that sound to you, Hatch?

Fine, he said. Please play your guitar tonight.

Why don't you ask your mother if it's okay with her?

Hatch looked at Mamma.

She was a long time in answering. I don't see why not.

Great. Blunt hammered a beat on the table with her roach-slaying palm.

After some time, she arranged herself in a chair with her guitar.

> *If you gon walk on my heart*
> *Please take off yo shoes*
> *Said, if you gon walk on my heart*
> *Kindly take off yo shoes*
> *I got miles to make up to you, baby*
> *And I ain't got no time to lose.*

Bright stringed music radiated from the sunburst guitar and enwebbed the entire room. Job done, the rays recoiled back into the dark sound hole.

Play another one!

Bedtime, Mamma said.

No it's not.

Bedtime.

It's too early.

Bedtime.

Fine.

Come on.

Fine.

Goodnight, Hatch. Blunt kissed him.

Goodnight.

He stalked out of the room. Pounced upon Mamma's bed and clawed the sheets. Voices on the other side of the glassed door tamed his anger.

I asked you.

I'm sorry.

I mean —

I really am sorry.

I explained my reasons.

Yes. He is a child.

I mean, you know plenty. What was that one the preacher liked?

Unchanging Hand.

Yes. How about that one?

A solid choice.

I've tried. Tried my best. I've been patient. More than patient. I'm not one to cry over spoiled milk.

No you aren't. And bless you for it. If you put spoiled milk in the refrigerator at night, it'll still be spoiled in the morning.

Yes.

Oh, Joy, I know. You may not believe it but I know. You see, I ain't much to look at. No feast for the eye. But the preacher chose me.

He wasn't a perfect man himself.

No he wasn't, but he was a good man . . . sometimes you had to fish for it. And good fish stay deep. Only the dead ones float on top.

Well, Mamma said. One might look at it that way.

Spoiled milk and dead fish both stink.

That's true.

Goodnight, Joy. Daughter.

Goodnight, Blunt. Mother.

THE NEXT MORNING HATCH ROSE EARLY and watched Mamma wake from the gray paralysis of sleep. She struggled out of bed, her hands positioned at her chest like a gloved surgeon, careful not to touch anything or let anything touch her. More than once he had watched her sore hands soak for hours in a deep tub of warm water and Epsom salt.

Mamma?

What?

Is Blunt sad?

What makes you think that?

Is she sad because the preacher died?

I don't know.

Is that why she can sing and stroke and make —

Don't talk that way.

I'm being frank.

You aren't being frank. Don't talk like that.

How come she likes to —

That's enough. Get ready for school.

They bathed and clothed, then entered the kitchen, the table set and breakfast prepared. Blunt followed her sweet heavy perfume into the room, tight leather jumpsuit and tall leather boots slowing and constricting her movement, and her makeup so thick she struggled to keep her chin up.

Goodmorning, Blunt.

Goodmorning, Joy.

Goodmorning, Hatch.

Goodmorning, Blunt. Blunt bent down — her eyes gray — and kissed him, then drew herself straight. In that space of time he glimpsed something in her face.

They all sat down at the round wood table.

Why are you dressed so early? Mamma asked.

I'm going out to buy some new guitar strings.

Mamma didn't say anything.

Maybe I'll even buy a new guitar.

Can you find you way around?

Sure. I'll take a cab.

Mamma, let Blunt take me to school today.

Remember your place.

No, Joy. It's okay.

No it's not okay. He's too smart for his own good.

That is so. How bout I take him to school today — if it's okay with you.

Mamma hesitated. Looked at Blunt. Looked at Hatch. Looked at Blunt again. Perhaps that would be good.

Blunt smiled.

I'll write down the address. Just show it to the driver.

Of course.

BLUNT SAT NEXT TO HIM LIKE A BIG BLOCK OF ICE in her white fur coat. The weather had not changed. For the first time, he was glad to be inside the padded snowsuit. Glad for Blunt's added fuzzy warmth. But he found it hard to keep still in his seat, victim to the stab of wonder. Should he confront her about what he thought he'd glimpsed in her eyes? Confront her about what he'd overheard last night? Something about dead fish, spoiled milk and funky smells. *Maybe she is a phony. Maybe she jus playin and singin to make me like her.* His curiosity caused him to sight down the guitar's polished neck, fret by fret — railroad tracks — to the ragged paper edge of a brown grocery bag; and to continue down the bag's side to a bottom corner and Blunt's black boot wedging it in place. *Why had she not brought the case along? Surely Mamma had noticed. Should he —*

How do you like school?

Just fine.

Of course you like it. You're a smart boy and you're doing so well. I'm proud of you.

Thank you.

I was real proud when you graduated from kindergarten.

Hatch said nothing.

That beautiful picture Joy sent me.

Yes.

And now we're all together.

Yes.

I'll buy that new guitar and play something nice for you this evening.

Fine. Will you play —

Maybe. Let's wait and see what your mother wants to hear.

Why did you put yo guitar in that bag?

Blunt didn't say anything for a moment. Why, didn't I jus tell you. I plan to sell it. A pawn shop, or the Salvation Army or something.

Why you leave yo case at home?

I don't need it.

Why you ain't jus throw it away?

Some people are needy.

You want to help the needy people?

Yes.

So you want needy people to have your guitar?

Yes.

Why?

Because —

Let me have it.

Oh. You don't want this old thing.

Why not?

It barely plays.

I thought you said you said you gon teach me how to play?

Yes.

Then I can use that old thing.

I'll buy you a nice new one.

Fine.

But —

Fine.

Wouldn't you like a new guitar?

Sure, he said. But you ain't gon buy it, he thought.

Enjoy school, Blunt said. She kissed him on the cheek.

I will, he said. Her pug nose looked like a big beetle stuck to her face.

Goodbye, Hatch.

Goodbye, Blunt.

WHERE'S BLUNT?

Plumed exhaust rose from the idling cab.

She hasn't returned. Mamma spoke from the dark, cavelike insides.

She was sposed to pick me up.

Mamma blinked nervously. Did she say that?

No.

Well.

I thought she was gon pick me up.

Watch your mouth. Those kids at this school are a bad influence.

She was sposed to pick me up.

Get in this cab.

He got inside the cab. The driver pulled away.

How come we can't take the train? He spoke to the moving window, the moving world.

We have no reason to take the train.

I'm being frank.

Please be quiet.

He obliged. Quiet and caught, the living moment before him and behind. He tried to image Blunt's face and received the taste of steel on his tongue. He let his violence flee like the soaring El cars above, a flock of steel birds rising out of a dark tunnel into bright air, and the city shrinking below.

The cab slowed and felled his desires. Slim currents of traffic congealed into a thick pool up ahead. The taxi advanced an inch or two every few minutes. The El's skeletal structure rose several stories above them. An occasional train rumbled by and shook the cab and mocked his frail yearning. He looked out the window to vent his anger. A good ways off he could discern a woman standing in a building doorway, a guitar strapped to her body, and a soup can at her gym-shoed feet. Coatless in a checkered cotton dress, her bare muscular legs firm as the El's pylons in the bitter cold. She kept rhythm with one foot, while some lensed smiling face rose or fell with each stroke of the guitar.

He shouldered the cab door open and started through the street, his boots breaking through snow at each step and traffic so thick he had to squeeze between the cars. Wind tried to push him back and the fat snowsuit wedged between two cars. But he freed himself from the moment and thought of his mother and thought of his father and thought of the preacher and thought of Blunt and fancy clothes and contact lenses and lahzonyah and smiles and promises.

Hatch! Mamma shouted after him, her voice distant, weak, deformed, small, dwarfish, alien. Intent on his target, he moved like a tank in his armored snowsuit, smooth heavy unstoppable anger. Close now. Blunt framed in the doorway, his face framed on her guitar. Her hair was not long and flowing and silver but knotted in a colorless bun. Her eyes were not green or blue or brown or gray, but a dull black. She shut them. Aimed her pug nose arrowlike at the El platform. Snapped open her mouth.

> *Baby baby, take off this heavy load*
> *Oh, baby baby lift up my heavy load*
> *Got this beast of burden*
> *And he got to go.*

Quick legs, he stepped up onto the curb and almost tilted over in the heavy snowsuit. He kicked the tin can like a football, coins rising and falling like metal snow, then crouched low and charged like a bull. He felt wood give under his head and loose splinters claw his face. He fought to keep his balance, loose coins under his feet, and in the same instant found himself flailing his hands and arms against Blunt's rubber-hard hips and legs. Gravity wrestled him down. Dazed, he shook his head clear, gathered himself in a scattering moment and looked up at Blunt. Her lined face. Her pug nose. Her stork mouth. And the strapped guitar that hung from her body — broken wood, twisted wire, useless metal — like some ship that had crashed into a lurking giant.

His eyes met hers, black, stunned. Wait, she said. You don't understand. She shook her head. You don't —

I hate you! he screamed. I hate you! Concrete shoved him to his feet. I hate you! Brutal wind pulled him into motion and led him as if leashed. Down the sidewalk, beyond the El's steel pylons, through warped, unfamiliar streets.

V

FORUM

BROADSTREET, DETROIT, MICHIGAN

Bridgett M. Davis

WHENEVER I VISIT MY SISTER IN DETROIT, I rent a car so that I can zoom along the city's freeways and streets and reconnect with the landmarks of my childhood. She lives downtown now, in a luxury high-rise apartment complex where the legendary Rosa Parks has come to spend her twilight days. My sister's apartment is dominated by wall-length windows that offer expansive views of the Detroit River — where barges drift lazily along the water, yachts dock, and Canada's skyline of casinos beckons. At night, lights twinkle off the Ambassador Bridge, casting elongated beams onto the black river. It's a stellar view, hypnotic and seductive — and it seldom holds my attention for more than a day.

Inevitably I find myself jumping into the brand new Chevy Cavalier or Pontiac Grand Am or Ford Probe I've rented and taking the Lodge Freeway northbound to Livernois Avenue, exiting, making a left, going a few blocks to Glendale, turning left, driving one block, turning left again, then slowly cruising past the spot where 12836 Broadstreet used to be.

Where the house I grew up in used to be.

It's gone now, the house. But I can conjure it back into existence by parking the car at the curb and simply staring at the hole where it once sat. That hole, that gap between what was and what never again will be, seems to get bigger each time I visit.

Imagine what it must have felt like for my mother back in 1960 when she strolled up the walkway and stepped onto the porch of the house on Broadstreet for the first time. Barely 32, and with a baby on her hip (me), she was about to take her family across the threshold from a tenuous existence to a secure future. Five years after arriving penniless in Detroit from down south, she and my father were about to purchase their first home. And not just any home, but a three-story, four-bedroom brick house on a wide, tree-lined avenue where the street lights popped on magically at dusk every evening. On the good side of town.

WHEN MY PARENTS FLED THEIR HOME IN TENNESSEE, they were part of the new wave of postwar migrants flooding the north from places below the Mason-Dixon line, escaping as fast as they could the last mean vestiges of Jim Crow and the south's low-paying, menial work. They'd heard about the good-paying jobs awaiting in the factories up north. It was 1955. They had real hope in their hearts. They believed things were changing. They settled initially in Pontiac, where my father had acquired work on the assembly line at General Motors. Within a year they moved to Detroit. Motor City was the place to be. Negroes could vote, drink from the same water fountains as whites, even sit beside them on a bus if they were so inclined.

Where they could live, however, was another matter.

Newly arriving blacks were relegated to just a few areas in the city. The poorest section was a small Lower East side neighborhood just east of downtown called Black Bottom, where blacks had lived since the beginning of the century. Just to the north was a densely populated area which migrants optimistically named Paradise Valley. It was anything but. While it had a thriving black cultural life, it also had old ramshackle tenements owned by absentee landlords, rashes of crime and rampant disease. Fire was an ever present danger.

My parents found a place to live on the other side of town — in a colored section on a narrow, rough street called Delaware, just off of Twelfth Street (the infamous street where the 1967 race riots would eventually break out). They suffered it out there for two horrible years in a cold-water flat, fighting overcrowding and the rats and roaches that came with it. There were four children by then, including a new baby, and things looked bleak. Like most Negroes, they rented from a white landlord who took advantage of the shortage of available housing for blacks in the city and charged them an exorbitant rent. Eviction was an ever present threat. While wages were good in the factories compared to what he'd left behind, my father, like many black men, was placed in one of the poorer-paying, less secure jobs at the plant. And the 30-mile commute to and from Pontiac was harsh. In those early years, they had no car. And the auto industry had already begun reducing employment in the Rust Belt cities, replacing workers with automated technology and constructing new facilities in other areas of the country and abroad, all of which would devastate Detroit in the years to come. Work for my father was not steady. He got laid off and rehired at the GM plant more than once. That, coupled with the fact that the rental market was small and overpriced, meant my parents were spending a larger percentage of their meager income on rent. The poorer you are, the more you pay.

EVEN TWENTY YEARS LATER, my mother would never drive anywhere near the vicinity of Delaware Street, because, she said, the memories were too painful. But that's all she would say. "They caught hell," is how my uncle John describes my parents' life on that street. "I went by to bring them some coal to heat the furnace and I was shocked. I told her to go back home; she didn't have to live like that," he says. "Our people had property."

My parents *were* poor, which is something they hadn't been in the south. And yet, despite the poverty, my mother wasn't budging. She had come from a family of enterprising black southerners who managed to own businesses and land, and she desperately wanted to own something too, but not in Nashville, Tennessee. Not down south. She wanted her children to grow up in a place where they didn't have to lower their eyes when a white person entered the room, or be called *boy* or *gal* or *niggra*. She didn't want her children to have to say "Yes, Ma'am" to every white woman they encountered. (In fact, we were not allowed to say "Ma'am" or "Sir" to *anyone*, black or white. "You're not on a plantation," my mother would snap. 'Yes' or 'No' will do just fine.")

What saved my family, I suspect, from the catch-22 cycle of endless poverty that has gripped so many African Americans was my grandparents' generosity. One desperate day in 1958, my mother called her own mother in Nashville and told her she needed help, and my grandparents — who had nine grown children by then — sent her $900.

That money helped my parents to "get on their feet" as they say, and they were able to move to a four-family flat on Clarendon Street, in a cleaner, working-class colored neighborhood. My mother often told the story of how her landlord — a black man named Mr. Saddlewhite — saw her planting flowers and grass in the front yard of the flat and confessed to her that he also owned the two-family flat across the street. He told her he liked how she took care of his property and that if she could swing the $75 a month rent, the better place was hers. They couldn't afford it, but she took the place anyway. It was bigger, and the family was growing. My father began moonlighting as a house painter, and they managed to make their payments. They had another baby. Things were better. They might have remained on Clarendon for many years (some of their friends actually did), and we may never have known life on Broadstreet had my mother not hit the number.

*T*HAT HIT GAVE MY PARENTS THE DOWN PAYMENT for a real home. I smiled when I read in Colin Powell's autobiography that his father bought their family's home the exact same way. In many black communities, hitting the number (the illegal precursor to winning the lottery) is the equivalent of borrowing a hefty sum from Mom & Dad, or pulling down an investment or using the nest egg.

That influx of cash changed the course of our family's fate. At best it would have taken several years for my parents to save the money for a down payment — years which, it turns out, my father couldn't spare because within a few years after they moved into the house on Broadstreet his health began to fail him and he found himself unable to work. Plus, even though there were affordable houses in Detroit, they were primarily in all-white neighborhoods, and black residents were shut out of the private real estate market. Realtors enforced "covenants" to keep white neighborhoods "homogeneous" — particularly those in affordable, working-class areas. Besides, bankers seldom lent to black home buyers, and they were abetted by the Federal housing appraisal practices that ruled black neighborhoods to be dangerous risks for mortgage subsidies and home loans. That meant that most blacks were trapped in the city's poorer housing in the strictly segregated areas. And that would have included my family if it hadn't been for our windfall.

Still, even with the money, it wasn't easy. My father had only been at the Pontiac plant for six on-again off-again years and was considered high risk by home sellers who didn't want to hedge their bets on unstable Negroes. My parents had to rely on the good graces of an older family friend who had been working in the auto plants for several years and who had good credit. He actually "bought" the upscale house on Broadstreet — which cost $16,500 — then quick-deeded it to my parents, who then took over the mortgage through a land contract. Land contracts were commonplace for black homeowners because they circumvented banks and mortgage lenders. It required a heftier down payment — in my parent's case, 30 percent — higher interest rates and, since the owner held onto the title until the balance was paid, also meant my parents had no equity in their home until it was paid for. Still, it was better than not owning at all. And so every month Mr. Prince, the man who sold his house to my parents (via the third party), would come to our home and collect his $135 mortgage payment. He was one of only two white people whom I can remember ever gracing our doorway. (The other was my sister's French tutor.) Mr. Prince paid the annual property taxes on the house; so he'd add that expense to the outstanding balance — until it dawned on my mother that at that rate they'd never own the home outright, and so she extricated herself and my father from that arrangement. All in all, even though Mr. Prince took his chimed bells with him when he moved out, my mother had no harsh words for him. He'd sold his house to her. And she soon bought her own chimed bells, which sang out in harmony every time the doorbell rang. I will never forget those three distinct notes — *dinggggg, donggggg, dingggg.*

M**R. PRINCE WAS TYPICAL OF MANY WHITE DETROITERS** trekking to the suburbs back then. Ironically, because he was part of the white-collar, upper-middle class, he and his neighbors were willing to sell their homes to black buyers. The house on Broadstreet was located in a neighborhood known as Russell Woods in the city's northwest section, and it's where clerks, engineers, accountants, midlevel white-collar workers and businessmen like Mr. Prince lived. All of the houses were substantial three- and four-bedroom brick homes designed to be small-scale versions of the more elaborate houses of the auto execs and bankers and doctors and lawyers who lived in tonier neighborhoods throughout the city.

It was inevitable that by 1960 blacks would eventually win the right to live in neighborhoods beyond those segregated borders imposed upon them: the Detroit chapter of the NAACP was the largest in the nation, black ministers were speaking out on housing issues, and the black vote was being felt by Democratic politicians. And so while whites in working-class communities fought bitter battles to keep blacks out — mounting organized, grassroots campaigns that relied on everything from hysteria to intimidation to violent harassment — those whites who could afford to move did just that, fleeing to ranch-style houses with attached garages in suburban places like Southfield and Birmingham and leaving behind a pool of quality houses that blacks could now buy. White flight created many long-term disadvantages for Detroit as a whole, but for individual black families like my own it gave us a shot at a lovely home in a nice, mixed neighborhood.

A mixed neighborhood was important to my mother. She'd considered purchasing a home in Conant Gardens, the all-black enclave of upper- and middle-class black residents — the doctors, ministers, funeral parlor owners and lawyers — who lived in mostly new houses on the city's northeast side. But in the end she opted against it. She had little use for separate but equal. When we moved to Broadstreet, we had black neighbors, Native American neighbors and some who were white, including our next-door neighbors, whose daughter Suzy played with me in our backyards before either of us understood what a social experiment our making mud pies together actually was. My mother believed in integration, believed that the key to hard-fought equality was the right for the races to live together side-by-side, because she understood from her southern roots a basic principle: that where there was a white presence, there would be amenities. She wanted quality grocery stores and roads that got repaired and street lights that worked and garbage that got collected regularly. She believed that as long as I sat beside white classmates in a public school, I'd receive a decent education. And for a handful of years it worked that way, until 90 percent of the city's white population — having lost the open-housing battle, and convinced that a black presence lowered property values — abandoned Detroit, unwilling to live beside its black citizens. Those who remained couldn't afford to leave.

BROADSTREET STRETCHES FOR ONLY TEN BLOCKS in its entirety — from Davison Avenue to Joy Road. Russell Woods Park is three blocks from where our house was. Back then the park had wooden benches, lush foliage and picnic tables. There were free concerts in the summer when bands came to perform. Winterhalter Elementary and Junior High School, which my sister and I attended, is just four blocks away. Each house on our block was distinctive, designed by a different architect. Where one is a mock French chateaux, another is Tudor style. Still another replicates the formal Georgian estates, while ours was more like a New England-style colonial. The house had innumerable details and lovely features like stucco walls, double French doors leading to the dining room and the den and windows adorned with stained glass. We had a breakfast nook, a modern basement with a bar and a spacious backyard. And the neighborhood was safe. Diana Ross and the Supremes each owned a house just two blocks away, on Buena Vista. We knew we were living well. We knew too that many black people weren't so lucky. Gratitude permeated the house along with the smell of catfish frying on the stove. Our big bustling house became a hub — for relatives from down south who came to visit regularly in order to see how Fannie and John T. had "made it" up north, for friends of my siblings who were falling on hard times and sometimes for the neighborhood teens who had reasons for not wanting to go home at night.

The street had been appropriately named. For a residential street, it is wide and busy. Two-way traffic flew by our house regularly since Broadstreet is an artery connecting two main thoroughfares in the city. My sister and I would often sit on the spacious front porch and play "My Car, Your Car" with our friends. When a car would whiz past, it was your car if you could name it; and the next one was mine if I could name it. The fun of it was getting the new cars while your opponent got the old clunkers. We learned the make and style of most American-made cars that way.

*L*IFE ON BROADSTREET EXPANDED MY HORIZONS. The pride my parents felt about the house trickled down, and I began to imagine great things for my life. There was something about the physical space of the house, the different floors, the many rooms, the sprawling front and back yards, the secret nooks and crannies — that gave me, as a child, a sense of possibility. I'd climb the creaky steps to the attic and daydream about the places I'd visit one day as I studied the tree tops from my own little paned-glass window. I'd hide in a corner of the back room in the basement with my writing paper and crayons and invent stories about people I'd never met. And I'd lie prostrate on the huge backyard lawn and stare up at the sky, secure behind my family's protective fence, imagining what a plane ride through the clouds would be like. I know you can dream from small, crowded places. But it's harder. Space allows you private time, a way to stretch your mind along with your legs.

We lived together as a family in that house throughout the decade of the 60s, a time when much of Detroit was being invaded by the ills of urban neglect. We felt insulated from most of that because of where we lived in the city, which is why to this day I always brace myself whenever someone asks where I'm from. I say "Detroit," and the person looks at me with sympathy or incredulity, eyebrows arched. "Really?" is usually the response I get. This annoys me. I am grateful that my parents moved to Detroit and proud that they managed from meager blue-collar beginnings to acquire a middle-class life. The house on Broadstreet was an obvious symbol of their American dream come true: French Provincial living-room furniture, color TVs, plush red carpet throughout, swing sets in the backyard and genuine china in the china cabinet. Living well gave their children the incentive to do well. And great things started to happen. Graduation pictures began to collect atop the mantle above the fireplace. My sister became one of the few blacks to be accepted to Wayne State University. Eventually all four of my parents' daughters attended college — the first generation in the family to do so.

Of course, it was the 60s, and no matter where we lived we couldn't be completely insulated from the turbulence of the times. Things came to a head in the city on a hot July night in 1967. In the middle of a summer heat wave, when unemployment for young black men was between twenty-five and thirty percent, a race riot erupted on Twelfth Street after police busted a "blind pig," an illegal after-hours joint. Tempers rose, the crowd grew, somebody threw a bottle at a police officer, and chaos ensued. Looting and burning thrived for five days. When it was over, forty-three people were dead, and Twelfth Street and its environs were in ruins. It would take years and years before most of the burned-out streets would be rebuilt (some never were), and Twelfth Street would be renamed Rosa Parks Boulevard. During the riot rumors flew that Russell Woods, just a few blocks from our house, was going to be set on fire. We were terrified of losing our home. My parents stayed awake each of those five nights, my father keeping watch in the front window, guarding the house from angry rioters with nothing to lose. Our family had everything to lose. My father was prepared to stand down a mob if he had to, because he understood that nothing so cruelly mocks hard-won gains in life than a fire to your home.

*I*N 1969 MY PARENTS DIVORCED AMICABLY, and my mother moved us younger children further north in the city to an area called Sherwood Forest — where once upon a time white Detroiters of means had lived, and where navy blue signs dotted telephone poles announcing that the streets were "privately patrolled." That house, on West Seven Mile Road, was the complete opposite of the one we'd left behind. It was modern, with stylish gray brick, double front doors with giant brass knobs in their centers, all the rooms on one floor and a huge picture window looking out onto a street where four lanes of traffic flew by. Still, the house on Broadstreet remained our real home, with various family members living there over the years, at different junctures in our lives. I even returned to it briefly in 1983, following a year traveling abroad.

My mother sold the house on Broadstreet in 1989. Three years before, a fire caused major damage to it. She offered it for very little money to a young man who wanted to renovate it and move his family into it. But he too eventually sold it, and a few years later another fire damaged the house beyond repair. Both fires had been started by embittered, jealous husbands — one my own brother-in-law. In 1994 the city chose to raze the house. And now there's just that giant gaping hole where our family's history used to be.

When I drive by and park my rental car in front, a part of me is grateful that my mother didn't live to see what became of 12836 Broadstreet. **v̇**

"M/orality"

Wayne Koestenbaum

16 OCTOBER 1998. Met President Clinton in the Oval Office. Gave him advice. Told him I admired his illicit sex. He smiled, eyes crinkly.

Told him I respected his oral adventures. Told him it was time a gay pundit spoke up on his behalf. Dubbed him the first queer President.

Called him Oscar Wilde. Read him extracts from *De Profundis*. Said the *fin de siècle* needed sexual martyrs. He volunteered.

He pretended to be interested in my speech. He put his head on my shoulder and inhaled the fumes of my assistance.

I tried to remember what Freud wrote about orality. Tried to make a point about oration, the mouth, longwindedness.

17 OCTOBER 1998. Told Clinton I liked his body. Told him it was an honor to experience it from afar.

He shook his head, almost in tears, but didn't tell me to stop talking.

Told Clinton that his face had a bruised appearance. Apologized for bruising him.

He gave me Woody Allen's phone number, said I should get a quote from Woody for the moral story I was writing.

Asked Clinton for an opinion about *Bowers v. Hardwick*. Reminded him of the case's details. Discussed sodomy. Tried to define it. Failed.

18 OCTOBER 1998. Told Clinton that he was a small boy. Called him perverse. He said no.

Thanked him for *déjà vu*.

Told him I wanted back the word "moral."

Advised him to stop bragging about God and the Bible and church-going.

Mrs Clinton entered the office, saw us, said "Excuse me, I'll leave you boys alone," shut the door. She was tough: she didn't care what he did with his body.

I said, "I don't want to take advantage of her good mood."

What about Mrs Clinton's feelings? I began to worry about her point of view.

19 OCTOBER 1998. I hope my White House days last forever.

Clinton was glad I used the word "blowjob," a beautiful coinage.

Told him our conversations were counterphobic counterespionage.

He laughed.

Told him I was serious.

He said he knew my reputation for gravity.

Relished the President's transparency.

20 OCTOBER 1998. Asked Clinton if I could read his diary. He said he didn't keep one; he didn't have time to write things down. He travels at the speed of light.

Showed Clinton a suitcase full of porn I carry with me at all times. We laughed at the pictures, but we didn't laugh at our nostalgia.

Asked him about photography. Demolished his chance for divine election.

21 OCTOBER 1998. Clinton asked if I liked the hotel. I said the towels were rough; they abraded my skin. He was no longer listening. My voice trailed off.

Complimented his sexual inventiveness. Praised the cigar. Tried to be subtle. Told him that sex was old hat: he'd made it new. He bristled. I'd gone too far?

Told him I had a soft spot for the sexually humiliated. Again he looked weepy. Told him I planned to reorganize my schedule around his greatness.

22 OCTOBER 1998. My pass rebuffed.

I'm resigned to his heterosexuality.

Clicked on a microcassette recorder to tape our conversations.

Promised Clinton I wouldn't sell the tapes.

Told him I was recording all my chats — not just White House ones — for a research project on flow and humiliation. I want to chart the movements up and down of a voice confessing or refusing to confess.

Silently admired his beefy chest. Tried to figure out whether he was a boy or a man, and why it mattered.

23 OCTOBER 1998. Massaged Clinton's shoulders. Removed a kink.

Praised his dorsal development.

Speculated about Jefferson and Sally Hemmings.

Asked Clinton the source of his fortune. A minion in the hallway hissed, "He's not rich!"

Mentioned failing health, faith healing.

24 OCTOBER 1998. Told him I prayed he wouldn't be punished.

Told him he deserved praise.

"For my humanity," he continued.

Talked McCarthyism, remembered Lillian Hellman, wished she were alive. Didn't mention Lillian's lies.

Explained Foucault to the President. Mentioned surveillance. Plotted resistance.

Clinton grew gleeful.

Read him extracts from Wilde's fairy tales.

"If only I were saying these things about myself," Clinton said, as if to himself.

25 OCTOBER 1998. Again propositioned Clinton. He refused.

He agreed, however, to watch.

So I called a service, requested an escort. Sam arrived. Husky and surly.

Sam blew me in a corner. I pilfered a climax. Clinton watched.

Was I dehumanizing Sam?

Later, at a party, Rosemary Woods accused me of idealism.

I am accustomed to accusation.

26 OCTOBER 1998. Asked Clinton for advice on growing older. He said he couldn't remember age forty. His mind grew vague. "Focus, focus," I demanded. He told me that decades were sad photographic negatives of earlier decades.

Took his picture.

He called me "tendentious."

He agreed that we were cognates.

I was doing most of the work, but I would give him half the credit for our revelations.

27 OCTOBER 1998. We comforted each other with Al-Anon slogans.

A rash below my right eye: what does it signify? Clinton said sometimes disease doesn't mean anything.

Told him not to trust his euphoria.

28 OCTOBER 1998. Told him our intimacy must soon end. He accused me of faithlessness.

He came to my hotel and sat by the side of the tub while I soaked. He held my hand and I tried not to splash water on his suit, on his legalese.

Witches don't float: my body settled at the bottom of the tub.

He asked me to make a fist. He admired my biceps.

"The political is," he began, and hesitated: "is or is not personal?" He remembered feminism, forgot it, chewed his lower lip.

The Secret Service took him away.

29 OCTOBER 1998. He swiveled in his chair, as if to offer me his body.

"You're not very imaginative," he said.

He meant my approach to incarnation.

I played with the objects on his desk. I played with the paper clips. I played with the stapler. I played with the secretary when she entered and I played with the President when she exited.

"Purchases can't save your life," he cautioned.

He was supposedly capitalism's avatar. Was he now a turncoat?

30 OCTOBER 1998. Thanked him for tormenting my senses: spirit nerves palpated by the President.

"Why cherish overstimulation?" he asked. And then: "Why scape-goat it?"

I read him the poem about the unknown soldier.

We attempted to do a few true things together, some corporeal.

He promised to write a saxophone and piano duet for the two of us to perform.

He promised to drive to Arlington with me in an armored car.

On the way he would tell me his plans for the next century.

I would help him bring these plans to fruition.

31 OCTOBER 1998. He advised me to call the diary a fable.

"But it's true," I said.

He listened, enjoying my sadistic gibes.

The Oval Office's openness depressed me.

"Shouldn't there be guards?" I asked.

"No prison strong enough that love can't force an entrance," he offered.

He called me his "little bastard": a friend of the family.

"Are you immoral?" I asked.

"Bad?" he rehearsed, mishearing. He was searching for a key word. "Bad" unlocked some doors. Why not try it on every gate?

Mrs Clinton entered to discuss disgrace — its procedures, its secret advantages. I turned away, disguising my face, pretending to be someone else.

She mistook me for a reporter scribbling on a steno pad.

After she left, I thanked the President for letting me invade his privacy. Told him that I stood for moral causes. Told him that his body was sacred. Told him that it was moral to wish for the momentary obliteration that arousal offered. Assured him that blowjobs were their own absolution. Reminded him of sodomy's ancient dignity. Celebrated his sodomitical awakening. Tried to persuade him not to mend his ways. Promised that if we ever saw each other on the street, I'd pretend not to recognize him and wouldn't force on him the memory of our acquaintance. Thanked him for smashing my ego. Blessed him for erasing me. Told him the nation loved his body, respected its wherewithal. Reminded him that God was sexually errant. Persuaded him that God was the author of wandering. Told him that God wasn't part of my vocabulary but I wanted to communicate with the President by borrowing theological terms. Thanked him for pillow talk. Was too profuse in my thanks. Said farewell. Gave him a deep, Taoist hug, like Robin Williams and Matt Damon in *Good Will Hunting*.

Checked out of the hotel.

Revised my estimate of his sexual magnetism. Indeed, I've exaggerated it.

I NOVEMBER 1998. Clinton incommunicado. My pathos no longer interests him. Without the possibility of ever again speaking to him I am flooded with fragments of our afternoons:

The President as I felt him through his pants or as I imagined him.

His flat face, few features.

His poverty.

President as hobo.

President as naked wretch.

My knowledge that I could decimate him.

Even when he whispers, he is shouting.

The door always shut to Mrs Clinton. Why am I more precious than she?

My moral staunchness.

His choice of me as confidante and confessor.

His lie: "I love you."

His quick abandonment of what he said yesterday.

My mouth.

The rules of time he broke.

Softness and availability of my breast in the Oval Office afternoon.

Sex disgusts me, but I swallow the disgust.

Later, the disgust returns.

He asked why I repeat the disgust if I dislike it.

I replied: disgust refines consciousness.

He called my mind inferior.

I watched his infraction and excused it.

He watched me watching. He sucked my omniscience. He had none of his own.

What's in a Place? What's in a Name?

Leo Ou-fan Lee

Always, from my earliest remembered days, I longed above all to be —
to use once more a phrase to which I remain (perhaps excessively)
attached — worthy of the world. To this end I was fully prepared to
be tested, to perform labors. I began to learn about the heroes of
Greece and Rome through Nathaniel Hawthorne's *Tanglewood Tales*,
and of Camelot I became aware thanks to MGM's *Knights of the Round
Table*, starring Robert Taylor as Lancelot and Mel Ferrer as Arthur, and as
Guinevere, if memory serves, the incomparable Ava, that palindromic
goddess who looked just as good when seen from the back as from
the front.

— Salman Rushdie, *The Ground Beneath Her Feet*

ALF WAY THROUGH READING Salman Rushdie's new novel, *The Ground Beneath Her Feet*, I found myself hopelessly lost in my own nostalgia. His Bombay becomes my Shanghai; his characters in their adolescent revolt become mythic reincarnations of my own youth. He speaks the truth of my youthful sentiment in the passage above. "To be worthy of the world" of which I knew nothing beyond what I had learned from Hollywood movies.

I am far more attracted to Bombay than to London or New York. How is this possible? Why do I, a Chinese academic now teaching in the United States, feel so much at home in Rushdie's Bombay, circa 1960? Aside from our similar age, we have nothing in common. Yet, curiously, Rushdie's new novel has recalled my own past. I was born in China but grew up in a small town in Taiwan, called Hsinchu ("new bamboo"), a windy town where I spent eight long years of my youth trying to grow up fast and leave, to go to America. Rushdie's first several chapters capture the restlessness of my generation with such authenticity (can I still use this word?) that they remind me of the early films of the Taiwanese director Hou Hsio-hsien (*A Time to Live and a Time to Die; Dust in the Wind*).

YES, MEMORY SERVES YOU WELL, SALMAN, that is indeed the incomparable Ava Gardner, who also starred with Stewart Granger in *Bhowani Junction*, another MGM film which introduced me, for the first time in my life, to contemporary India. Yes, we shared another favorite in common, *Scaramouche*, in which Stewart Granger dressed like Beau Brummel (another film he starred in) performed some spectacular acrobatic feats fencing with the ever elegant Mel Ferrer in "the longest sword fight in movie history" — for more than twenty minutes, if memory serves. The same Mel Ferrer, who would soon be King Arthur, played an 18th-century French aristocrat (who turned out to be Scaramouche's lost brother, like Virus to Ormus Cara in your novel) before he married another of my goddesses, Audrey Hepburn, in real life. Oh, these MGM spectaculars, how they dominated the imagination of youths across the globe! We probably watched them around the same time in the mid-1950s: you in the deluxe Metro cinema in downtown Bombay, I in a dingy little theater in Hsinchu, called Guomin daxieyuan (Grand Theater of National People) where I spent practically every weekend spellbound by these mythologies of the celluloid. The satanic allure of American capitalism, the commodified poison of people of the Third World or the stuff of which our jejeune fantasies are made of and against which our puerile strivings toward imagined manhood were tested?

I WRITE THE ABOVE AS I THINK OF YOUR REVEALING STATEMENT: "What deflects us from the subject is loss. Of those we love, of the Orient, of hope, of our place in the book. Loss is more than love or is it. More than death or is it. More than art, or not." What we cherish in nostalgia is also loss — the loss of a bygone era that seems eternal because it is so ephemeral — except that in your novel this bygone era seems to be lost forever.

> *I am writing here about the end of something, not just the end of a phase of my life but the end of my connection with a country, my country of origin as we say now, my home country I was brought up to say, India. I am trying to say goodbye, goodbye again, goodbye a quarter century after I physically left. This ending is oddly positioned, coming as it does in the middle of my story, but without it the second half of my life could not have happened as it did. Also, it takes time to come to terms with the truth: that what's over is over. Because as it happens I did not go of my own free will. As it happens I was driven out, like a dog. I had to run for my life.*

A plain paragraph, to be sure, yet I detect so much elegiac poignancy beneath it! Without the first half (set in Bombay) the second half of the story (ranging across rock music scenes in England and America) could not have happened as it did. It also made me think of the title of another famous essay of yours, "Imaginary Homelands": Has India become "imaginary" precisely because it is the country you have left? Why are you saying goodbye again and again to the homeland of your imagination, the homeland that still fuels your imagination? Why don't you simply leave her behind? It seems the farther the characters in the novel want to get away the closer they are bound to Bombay — to the "ground beneath her feet."

ON MY FIRST VISIT TO INDIA IN DECEMBER 1997, I made the impulsive decision after attending an academic conference in Delhi to fly all the way to Bombay just to see with my own eyes the old Art Deco movie theaters. As I stood in front of Eros — all worn-out now, like aged Ava, but still imparting an irresistible aura — I thought of the old Grand Theater (Daguangming) in Shanghai, which I wrote up in *Shanghai Modern*. This theater was renovated in 1933 to Art Deco splendor by the renowned Czech architect Ladislaus Hudec complete with two thousand sofalike seats — each equipped with earphones for simultaneous translation — a marbled lobby, three fountains, a huge neon-lit marquee and fancy restrooms painted in light green. I first became curious about Bombay when some years ago I gave a lecture in Chicago on Shanghai architecture, and a colleague there told me about the "Bombay style" — or *Art dekko* which Bombay claimed as its own. Shanghai in the 1930s also claimed to own the largest number of Art Deco buildings — including movie palaces and skyscrapers — in Asia. Most of the movie palaces were situated in Shanghai's International Settlement, whose colonial names — Odeon, Strand, Empire, Victoria and Carlton — must have carried a familiar ring to Bombay residents. I see these two cities, in hindsight, as "twin sisters" whose old cosmopolitan grandeur has paved the historical ground for the rise of a new "vernacular cosmopolitanism" today (to use a term coined by Homi Bhabha, a Parsi intellectual from Bombay). Shanghai's modernity has a cultural genealogy all its own which has been forcibly erased by Chinese socialism for nearly half a century. In fact it was only a couple of years ago that Shanghai residents rediscovered the glory of their city's past, as they scratched the drab paint on the walls of the Shanghai and Hong Kong Bank building and found eight large murals depicting the world's eight greatest cities, including Shanghai. Now the entire city is possessed by a collective nostalgic mania: it seems that the city purposely embraces its past in order to assert its new identity as a world-class metropolis.

On the eve of my departure, I took a walk along Bombay's famed shoreline, the long embankment along Marine Drive, and was dazzled by the glitter of the new high-rise apartments. My guides were two friends, Dilip Gaonkar, an American academic originally from Bombay, and Kiran Nagakar, a most talented writer (*Raven* and *Eddie Cuckold*) who also writes in English and deserves to be better known internationally. They both told me that some of the buildings in this swanky area belonged to the Rushdie family. I now find reconfirmation in the novel: perhaps some were built by Ameer Merchant, the narrator's mother? Or am I irresponsibly confusing fact and fiction?

The conspicuous rise of the *nouveau riche* in present-day Bombay made a tourist like me all the more aware of the dilapidated state of the old colonial buildings, which looked particularly deserted on that Sunday. I was told that some radical critics in India had argued that they should be destroyed because they were built by British colonialism. If so, the Indian anti-colonists are not too far apart from the Chinese modernizers who also wish to destroy the old in order to hasten arrival of the new. The Communist regime in China has already dismantled the old city walls in Beijing and now threatens to raze more old buildings in the name of modernization.

Still, I am glad that a few old movie theaters remain. Shanghai's Grand Theater has undergone yet another renovation, thereby losing most of its old-world charm. But the Peace Hotel on the Bund, which used to be the old Cathay house owned by the Sassoon family (who also once owned property in Bombay), has been carefully refurbished to its old glory with all its Art Deco interiors intact. The Guomin Theater in

Hsinchu is now preserved as a "historical treasure" by order of the city government. I had a picture taken there, as I did in front of the Eros, and for no apparent reason thought of another MGM spectacular I had seen, *Gone with the Wind*. Hsinchu — Shanghai — Bombay: here is a new (or old) trajectory for further reflection, or for a further twist in postcolonial theory.

WHAT LIES BENEATH THE GROUND OF RUSHDIE'S BOMBAY — "the ground beneath her feet"? Besides memories I find mythologies profusely strewn around all the characters. Hovering over them all is the myth of Orpheus, the god of music and patron saint of singing. The name hits a nerve, for I can honestly claim that there is no other Chinese more attuned to Orpheus than myself. I say this for a personal reason: my real name in Chinese is Orpheus!

Imagine the emotional state of a young man in Hsinchu who, upon reading a Chinese translation of Edith Hamilton's *Greek Mythology* (instead of Nathaniel Hawthorne's *Tanglewood Tales*) on a languid summer afternoon suddenly felt the ground shaking beneath his feet — a new earthquake, like the one in Bombay in 1960 — as he found out for the first time in his life the full symbolic meaning of his name. He had no idea how his parents had chosen for their first-born son the name with a trilingual pun. To begin with, Ou-fan is a Chinese transliteration of Orphée or Orfeo, the French and Italian names of Orpheus. Confronted with this moment of truth, what could he possibly do? Make a big fuss in front of his parents or silently curse his own fate? Unlike Rushdie's daredevil protagonists, he chose to remain silent.

Still, a new idea began to gnaw at his heart: Where would his Eurydice be — in what disguise and speaking what language(s)? At the young age of sixteen, the age when Ormus Cama decides to sleep with Vina Apsara in the novel, our Chinese hero made two belated decisions in order to change his mythic fate: he vowed never to study music, instantly dropping his violin lessons and, as soon as he entered college, chose a new name for himself — Leo, after Leo Tolstoy, one of his favorite Western authors. (He came to Dostoevsky much later, after his new name was already stuck in his passport.)

I DID NOT TELL MY PARENTS ABOUT THIS SMALL DISCOVERY until years later. I had already anticipated their answer: they were fellow college students in Nanking when they met, both studying Western music. Besides, what's in a name anyway? They could afford to brag about its originality, that no one in China would ever think of using such a "foreign" name with such foreign-sounding characters? They did it for fun and, I now realize, for their own brand of cosmopolitanism, since the middle character of my name — *Ou* — also refers to Europe. My sister is named after America, my dead brother Asia and so on and so forth until the offspring round up all the five continents of the globe.

Thus at the tender age of sixteen I realized for the first time that I did not belong to China; even worse, I would be "alienated" forever. I didn't leave Taiwan because I was driven out; no, I left of my own free will, all because of my name, which doomed me to voluntary exile. Where then could be my "imaginary" homeland? Greece? Brazil (as in "Black Orpheus")? Or India? It so happens that the third Chinese character of my name, "*fan*," means Sanskrit, the ancient language of Indian Buddhism. Ou-fan: Europe/Orpheus/Sanskrit. The search for my mythic origins had inevitably led to a journey toward multiculturalism, long before the term was invented. Now that multiculturalism has become, even in theory, such a commonplace, I too have become common again. What seemed so exceptional and bizarre more than a quarter of a century ago has become the normal condition for all migrants and exiles, not to mention romantics and cosmopolitans around the world. I now realize why I feel such an affinity to Rushdie's novels, because they celebrate homelands and hybridities with an extraordinary multicultural imagination. After years of embarrassment and suffering — all because of my name — I now take heart from these poetic lines of Rilke as quoted in the novel's first page:

We should not trouble
about other names. Once and for all
it's Orpheus when there's singing.

So "let the rose bloom each year for his sake" — Orpheus or Orfeo, Vina or Ormus — wherever we are and wherever s/he is, in India or China. **V̇**

On the Anachronism of Poetry

Hugo Achugar

*I*S POETRY ANACHRONISTIC? It's possible the question is rhetorical, even absurd. It could also be the wrong way to put it.

I'll rephrase the question: To what extent is poetry still valid in contemporary society? Is it valid to speak about the "end of poetry" as it has been about the "end of art"? Do current cultural and technological changes as well as the rule of audiovisual culture allow us to even think the obsolescence of poetry? Obsolescence of all poetry or just a particular form or way of writing poetry? Perhaps what has become obsolete — even though poems continue to be read and consumed — is a precise way of doing poetry. Or is what's happening just another *corsi e ricorsi* in the history of modern art?

It's perhaps not by chance that I was asking these questions and wrote the major part of this essay before having read Hans Magnus Enzensberger's "Meditation on Anachronism" in the last issue of *Venue*. It seems that many of us in different parts of the world — Uruguay,

Mexico, Germany — are questioning the future of poetry. I do not know if I can agree with the prognosis that Jochen Hörisch — according to Enzensberger — made about the literary book but I do agree that "the future of the book of poems will depend upon its anachronism."

POETRY, FAR FROM BEING IN CRISIS, has seen how the number of poets and readers and listeners has grown over the last years. Thus, it is possible to affirm that the number of poetry readings, the number of poets or lyricists and songwriters — this new and old way to name poets — as well as the number of forms and ways of publishing or circulating poetry continues to grow. On the other hand, it has become commonplace to say that new artistic or poetic forms such as the videoclip have gained a growing place in the heaven of public preferences.

The anachronism of poetry may be the least of the problem. If literature itself is a relatively recent creation — linked to Modernity according to some, to the rise of nation-states and the idea of national literature according to others — and now is in crisis because of the explosion of mass media, poetry is even less prepared to resist the assault of the present, especially the cultural and media transformation.

Still… "Poetry continues to be read," the poets say in protest. That's true, partially. Poetry does continue to be read in the sense that some poems of some poets continue to be read. The problem is that when somebody makes an affirmation like "Poetry continues to be read," not everybody understands the same thing. Can we accept that a poem that accords with the notion of poetry sustained by high culture merely by virtue of being written in lines or rhyme and with a poetic intention, read perhaps by a teenager to his or her friend, is poetry? If by poetry we understand everything written with the intention of being poetry, then maybe poetry is still quite alive. But if intention, as we all know, is not enough and we ask for something more or something else, then the number of poets is dramatically reduced.

I am not arguing in favor of an elitist or academic view of poetry. I am just trying to figure out what we mean when we say "poetry." It is obvious that the way in which the Brazialian Haroldo de Campos's "spatial" poems and the Spaniard or Catalan Joan Brossa's "nonverbal" poems have abandoned the "traditional" way of doing poetry will not be accepted by the general public (the happy few that read poetry, I want to say) as poetry. This means — and there is nothing new about this — that poetry is an equivocal term.

*I*S IT SIMPLY, THEN, THAT THE KIND OF POETRY that prevailed during Modernity no longer finds general acceptance, is no longer in force? But that, too, has always been the case. Poetry has never been popular, at least in the sense that popular singers have been. The great examples of poetic success in Latin America, like *Martin Fierro* by José Hernández, belong to the 19th century, that is, to a pre-media past or to the kind of poetry that our great poets of Modernity wrote or promoted. And the poetry of tango or bolero or salsa singers is still not the kind of poetry that academics and high school teachers, cultural journals or literary prizes, recognize as desirable.

On the other hand, a different kind of poetry is quite alive. The recent Grammy awards ceremony was just another example of the emergence or reemergence of this new old kind of poetry; the lyrics sung in popular songs keep sending the old book of poems as Modernity conceived it back to the dusty shelves of libraries.

Maybe it is less difficult to understand why people still *write* poetry. On the one hand, it is a practice that goes back to the beginning of time. On the other, for a part of the society poetry is still a "prestigious" practice; some people still pronounce the word "poet" with a particular admiration. So, is poetry still current? Is it anachronistic? The answer, as always, varies according who tries to answer it and where. I believe it is anachronistic — as anachronistic as playing a violin or a harp, as anachronistic as flying in a balloon or using a canoe or even maybe writing with a goose quill.

It is possible, nevertheless, that in fifty or a hundred years even the question of poetry's anachronism will itself have lost meaning. The meaning of the word "poetry" may have to be sought in an ancient thesaurus. It's also possible, likely in fact, that poetry will be so different from what is still today practiced, especially as understood by "poets" from the "high culture" tradition themselves and by the people who recognize them as such, that nobody will be able to establish any kind of filiation between the old and the new form of art.

In order to be precise, what does not seem to be in force or to be prevailing is a certain kind of poetry, the kind which, in its diverse forms, most of us — rare dinosaurs — continue to write or to read. The problem is that most if not all "old high culture" poets do not get it, do not get that the future of poetry is elsewhere. And so far the future of poetry belongs to John Lennon, Lauryn Hill, Ricky Martin, Charlie Garcia, Jaime Roos, Sting and the like. There is no irony or malice in this prognosis. Actually, I am a fan of many lyric writers as well as of many "old high culture" poets. It is just that time is catching up with the uncontaminated realm of cultural activity known as poetry.

*F*INALLY, JUST BEFORE I PUT AN END TO THESE LINES I had the following thoughts.

In a sense poets and poetry have become like the ancient Christians in the "catacombs" of Rome. Poetry has become the secret ritual of an underground and elitist religion. Poets have become the priests, readers the believers, in a secluded rite for the initiated. If we believe that poets have become a sort of fundamentalist group defending their culture or religion in the face of the homogenization pursued by the media cultures, then their "anachronism" is not quite so. I mean, it could also be understood as a "resistance" to the evils of modern (or postmodern) times. Some might argue that it be understood as a persistence or trace of "primitive" culture that is simply dying hard.

On the verge of the new millennium, poetry might look like a sort of dinosaur just reborn in the Jurassic Park of contemporary culture. It could also therefore look extremely contemporary, for after all the other face of the globalized moon is the apotheosis of the singular, the local, the sect and the cult.

Jurassic anachronism or strict contemporaneity?

Both, I think.

Meanwhile, poets continue to gather in their catacombs practicing their heresy. Fundamentalists that they are, they entertain no doubts. They listen to the "fools" rhapsodizing in the music market and do not acknowledge these other contemporary poets. They do not realize that maybe music "videos" are the "poems" of these and the coming days. They continue to believe that "modern" or "avant-garde" poetry is all that there is to poetry and do not even dream they might be obsolete. In a way, it's fair to say it, they are a special kind of heroes or martyrs.

It's also fair to say that I am one of those contemporary-anachronistic dinosaurs. It is also fair to say that I cannot help it; I keep writing the old obsolete poetry I have been questioning. But that is not important. Compulsion never is.   V̇

Spirit and Flesh: Mexico's Sexual Revolution

Rubén Martínez

L ET'S BEGIN, SAFELY, WITH AN IDEA. An idea about a cata-
clysmic fuck, Mexico's big bang. Half a century ago, Octavio
Paz, Mexico's official bard (and finally, thankfully dead bard — he was
undeniably a great poet and essayist, but his intellectual deification strat-
ified Mexico's political life for several years) wrote of the "masks"
Mexicans have crafted over time, mythic identities whose function is to
hide the trauma of *"la chingada"* (from the verb *chingar*, "to fuck," lit-
erally and figuratively, as in "Fuck me, baby!" or "You fucked me over"),
that is, the conquest, which was essentially a sexual act — the rape of
native by conquistador from which modern Mexico's mestizo identity
was born. Now I don't agree with much else of what Paz wrote, and
although I am half-Mexican I don't feel I have to pay tribute to his bones
like every intellectual in Mexico City does, but I do think he had it right
with the idea of the masks.

Not surprisingly, the most common, and powerful, of the Mexican masks are sexual ones. The "macho" (hard-working, hard-drinking, hard-fucking) was necessary for Mexican men to regain some sense of manhood after *la chingada*. Likewise, the obsession with virginity imposed upon, and assimilated by, Mexican women was a way to purge the memory of primordial rape. The Catholic Church, true to its nature as a brutally patriarchal institution, played an important role in the formulation of this construct. But in the end, a mask is just a mask — it does not alter what lies behind it, although it can create a tension between myth and essence that results in comic, tragic and downright surreal acting-out. And in Mexico what lies behind the masks is a tremendous amount of fear, loathing and, of course, desire — of both self and other. Desire is always contradicting itself in Mexico, and it does so on every level — race, class, gender, sexual orientation, even religion. The homogeneity that Mexico presents to the outside world (indeed, even to itself through "official" culture), that of a uniformly brown and Catholic nation, is itself a mask that hides an exceedingly complex series of divides. The Indians hate and love the whites; the whites scorn and secretly desire the Indians; the mestizos cannot reconcile themselves with their liminality and so are attracted to and repelled by both white and Indian; the men revere and despise the women; the poor idolize the rich even as they dream of a second Mexican revolution to bring them down, and the rich romanticize the poor at the same time that they do everything they can to keep them in their place.

A ND SO MEXICO'S SEVERE SEXUAL CONTRADICTIONS. It is a most Catholic country where sex before and outside of marriage is officially a mortal sin — and a country where sex before and outside of marriage is rampant. A most "macho" country of rough and rowdy males whose reason for being is to conquer virginal señoritas — although these very men not only have a rich homoerotic fantasy life, but indulge it, in physical terms, to an amazing degree, and where the señoritas aren't virgins at all, in spite of the fact they make as great an effort as the machos to convince one of their authenticity. A country whose "family values" beat even those of Pat Robertson, with *mami, papi, abuelo* and *abuela* cutting mythic figures, with ma and grandma, especially, on saintly pedestals — and a country where most families exist in name only, with a rate of infidelity (in which those virginal women aren't far behind their macho partners) that results in the birth of millions of "illegitimate" children.

Mexico loves to fuck, in a Catholic way. It suffers its fucking so much (pecado mortal!) that its pain becomes a delight. We pick the forbidden fruit, we come, we realize the sin, we confess, we are given absolution, we pick it again. Psychologists, feminists and the French can complain all they want, but the fact is that it is precisely the fact that we've contradicted our desire that has made it so, well, sexy. Mexicans have not only become experts at the furtive fulfillment of desire, they have also perfected public sex. Dancehalls host all-night orgies where tropical rhythms cause groins to rub against each other unto stained jeans. The neo-primitives came late to the game: for centuries, Mexico City, as well as every provincial town and cowtown, has greeted the sun hungover and satiated — with everyone still fully clothed.

But not all sex is so safe. Central to Mexican sex are two masks — the *puta* and the *puto*, the whore and the fag, the most desired of all sexual personae. It is on the street, in the hotel room or at the *burdel* that the fiercest manifestation of Mexico's sexual contradictions takes place. It is the most desperate, the most lonely of fucks, sometimes accompanied by a violence that is the ultimate, terrible denial of what is a mythic void become physical, in which the tortured spirit seeks its salvation through burning flesh. This is not the kind of transubstantiation that Catholic theologians preach about, but then again, I've always thought that communion was suspiciously similar to oral sex.

There is a darkness inherent in the wearing of masks, and at times that darkness escapes the rote of the bedroom and runs dangerously out into the streets. During the early 90s in Mexico City, several dozen gay men were killed in a serial spree. The predators were police officers, the most macho of machos and, in Mexico's twisted sexual psyche, the most *puto* of *putos*. The cops were attempting to kill off in themselves that which they thought resided only in their victims.

*B*UT THE GAME OF THE MASKS, BOTH ITS LIGHT AND DARK SIDES, is changing in Mexico, and changing rapidly. Since December of 1994, Mexico has undergone its most severe crisis since the Revolution of 1910. There's been an Indian uprising in the south, a narco-war in the north, a peso devaluation that devastated the economies of both the capital and the provinces, a terrifying country-wide crime wave and an overall sense of identity crisis owing to the fact that millions of Mexicans are following the migrant route to the States and transforming the cultural landscape of their homeland in the process (NAFTA also helps out on this count). Mexico is on edge.

The collective hysteria has manifested itself in a spectacular split between spirit and flesh; Mexicans are simultaneously on spiritual and sexual quests. Mexico in recent years has been "re-sacrilized," experiencing a revival in both popular Catholicism (the Virgen de Guadalupe miraculously appears with increasing frequency these days, everywhere from migrant labor camps in the States to subway stops in Mexico City) and Pentecostalism, the insurgent religion giving *la Virgencita* a run for Her money. At the same time, Mexico has been "re-sexualized," desire becoming the most obvious metaphor for *la crisis* in Mexico today. Spirit, flesh: in the end the same quest, borne of a crumbling economy and identity.

The proliferation in prostitution, along with the tacit admission from the government to rein in the sex trade, is the single most apparent sign of crisis-sex, an "outing" of what has always existed, but furtively. Mexico City is busy not busting working women and men, but formulating legal and health guidelines for sexworkers. Also in vogue is the idea of official red light districts. In Tapachula, near the border with Guatemala, municipal authorities have created a city-within-a-city, replete with checkpoints for drugs and firearms and strict health codes that include regular STD checks. But these measures can only help prevent what has not yet occurred. AIDS has already arrived in Mexico, via tourists, and migrant men returning from their stints of work in the States, as well as having emerged from the very heart of the Mexican family, where the macho husband's liaisons with other men are no longer a secret.

Another sign is a shift away from the innocent dance-as-sex rituals toward the real thing. In Mexico City, sex clubs that once were underground operations now line Insurgentes Boulevard, the city's main north-south artery, gaudily announcing flesh in Vegas-style neon. At these clubs, table dancing is only the tamest of the entertainment. Live sex is increasingly common, and it's not the "vanilla" variety — there's something for virtually every proclivity: bisexual threesomes, S&M scenarios and toys, toys, toys.

Gay clubs are above ground now as well. Some 80 are said to exist in the downtown Cuahutemoc district of Mexico City alone. I have seen gay couples — men and women — holding hands, walking along the streets in broad daylight. Sex radicals would find much to celebrate in this very public reenactment of a John Rechy novel. But the crisis, economically and culturally, spiritually and sexually, has just begun. Right-wing Catholic and Pentecostal leaders are mounting an assault on the "immoral" plague. And then there is the private toll of this private contradiction gone public.

I LIVED IN MEXICO CITY FOR TWO YEARS, during a time that *la crisis* was already in high gear. Perhaps I should say that Mexico City lived me. The sex that I describe here is something I know because I myself indulged. I was swept up by what I experienced, initially, as the incredible eroticism of having all that's hidden and forbidden suddenly laid out before you, every secret desire and temptation. On more occasions than I'd care to count, I greeted the dawn under the influence of ever more volatile combinations of drugs and alcohol, my body tangled up in the body of another, in the bodies of others, my own gender and orientation as interchangeable as theirs. It was a territory where impulse reigned, where God knows what existential and historical echoes took the form of flesh. But, ironically, in the very instant of consummation I felt as if my body itself was being destroyed. I would crawl back to my apartment feeling like a ghost — a bodiless, terribly lonely spirit. Crisis-sex cannot affirm anything; it can only negate, for better or worse. I hadn't gone to Mexico searching for this kind of existential anonymity, but it is what the crisis bequeathed me. Mexico's crisis became my own.

I was dimly aware that I was walking through a fire that generations of Mexican men (the female experience of crisis-sex is, of course, altogether distinct) had already gone through, including my father, who, though he's never "outed" his own sexual secrets with me, I intuit experienced something similar when he lived in Mexico City as a teen in the 1950s. But crisis-sex is something even darker, and sadder, and even more frightening, than the sex Mexicans had long experienced behind their masks. For what is occurring in Mexico today is precisely the burning of all the masks. Mexico is coming out.

I don't care to ascribe any kind of morality to crisis-sex — let the Christian Coalitions of the world dwell on it (and there is one group in Mexico today, called *Pro-Vida*, that is well on its way to becoming a moral and political power broker of the most nefarious — read: American — kind). What I do want to say is that ultimately, my experiences of the senses, and of the senseless, in Mexico denied the body altogether. And I sense that I was not alone in this, that crisis-sex is less a manifestation of sexual liberation than it is of desperation, although — and this is the ironic silver lining — the very fact that the sexual is so "out" throughout Mexican society today does appear to be furthering the cause of tolerance in a land famously intolerant of otherness.

*F*OR AS THE FLESH IS MADE PUBLIC, inevitably questions arise. One did not discuss the patriarchal political economy of prostitution before *la crisis*, nor were misogyny and homophobia part of the discourse, nor did we talk of preventing STD's, or of bisexuality, or debate sex and love and whether the one exists without the other. A curious circle: we negate the body out of desperation, but it is resurrected instantly, precisely because it was our desperation that came out of the closet and was given form in the flesh, a private pain become excruciatingly and terrifyingly public. It's as if — and this is a quasi-Catholic notion — only by a journey into decadence could we realize that it was the spirit crying out all along.

There is another country being born here, a country that will always have its painful memory, but that perhaps can learn to live with its contradictions made public, its demons let loose, as it were, on the public square, where the Mexicans are fucking as never before.

ESSAYS

LORCA AND DALÍ

Leslie Stainton

1923-24

*E*verything Salvador Dalí did and said — his velvet coats and broad-brimmed hats, his manic pursuit of solitude, his brashly avant-garde work — was calculated to provoke admiration. When Lorca first set eyes on the painter, he had to disguise his amazement at Dalí's attire. The artist, in turn, was captivated by Lorca. He sensed at once that the olive-skinned Andalusian was somehow distinct from others at the Residencia in Madrid. During their first meeting, Dalí later recalled, "the poetic phenomenon in its entirety and 'in the raw' suddenly appeared before me in flesh and blood." As their friendship grew, Dalí became so smitten by Lorca's poetic "fires" that he had to work consciously to "extinguish" them with his own prosaic talk so as not to fall under the poet's sway.

Still, he found Lorca difficult to resist. Soon after their first encounter, the painter cut his hair, clipped his sideburns and bought a sports suit so that he could better fit into Lorca's crowd. He gave Lorca one of his paintings and sketched his portrait sitting in a café. The two engaged in long discussions about literature, art and aesthetics, often talking until dawn. At times they disagreed violently. But they always treated each other with sincerity, and Dalí came to rely on Lorca's superior knowledge of such matters as music. Once, at a concert, he inquired, "Should I be liking this?" Yes, Lorca said, and Dalí promptly burst into wild applause.

In many ways Lorca's antithesis, Dalí was so shy — despite his flamboyant appearance — as to be "almost mute," while Lorca was vigorous and outgoing, a font of laughter and music. Whenever Lorca took Dalí to a *tertulia*, the painter refrained from talking. Lorca reproached him for his reserve and devised a scheme for breaking the ice at such gatherings. "I'll say you're a great painter and that you're here working," he told Dalí.

But when silence descended in the midst of the next *tertulia*, Dalí panicked. Before Lorca could say anything, he blurted, "I'm also a very interesting painter."

On several occasions, Lorca took Dalí to dinner at the home of Residencia director Alberto Jiménez Fraud. As usual, Lorca talked and laughed through the evening, while Dalí kept to himself. When he did speak, it was with a deep, nervous voice and a heavy Catalan accent. He smiled rather than laughed, a furtive smile that exposed a row of tiny, sharp teeth. Jiménez Fraud's wife, Natalia, thought the artist "nothing more than Lorca's echo."

As the months wore on, Dalí shed his inhibitions. Shortly before the end of the spring 1923 term, he took part in a student protest at the Academy of Fine Arts and was expelled from school. Unrepentant, he went home to Catalonia, where he immediately took part in an illegal political demonstration and was sent to jail for a month. In prison, he bragged, "We drank lousy local champagne every evening."

1924-25

Hours after returning to Madrid that fall, Lorca read his ballads to a group of friends and admirers who crowded into his Residencia room to welcome him back to the capital. His face darkened by the summer sun, a stray lock of black hair on his forehead, Lorca leaned back in his bed and joyfully declaimed his gypsy poems. Among his listeners was Rafael Alberti, a twenty-one-year-old painter and poet from the Andalusian city of Cádiz, who thought Lorca looked like a peasant from the south.

That evening Lorca and Alberti dined together and afterward strolled through the Residencia gardens. There Lorca launched into a second, impromptu recital of his new poems. "Green, how I love you green," he intoned dramatically in the darkness. Alberti was struck by his warmth and spontaneity. At one point Lorca turned to Alberti and impulsively asked the handsome young poet to create a painting, one with a likeness of the Virgin beside a stream, and the legend "Apparition of Our Lady of Beautiful Love to the poet Federico García Lorca." Alberti was flattered. By the time the two parted, well after midnight, a soft rain had begun to fall. "Goodbye, cousin," Lorca said.

A few days later Alberti returned to the Residencia bearing the painting Lorca had requested, as well as a sonnet, "To Federico García Lorca, Poet of Granada." Lorca waved his hands effusively and told Alberti, "You've got two things going for you as a poet: a great memory and the fact that you're Andalusian."

Within a year of meeting Lorca, Alberti admitted to him that he felt like his "younger brother," and he suggested they stay in close touch with each other by letter. He became a regular visitor at the Residencia — one of dozens of young men pulled irresistibly into Lorca's orbit.

In Madrid, Lorca continued to work on his ballad series. His new roommate at the Residencia, José Rubio Sacristán, a law student, remembered that one winter night Lorca lay in bed with the covers pulled up to his neck and his fingers poking out from the blankets, scribbling onto a sheet of paper. The window was open — it was thought admirable at the Residencia to endure extremes of cold and heat — but despite the chill, Lorca pushed on, scratching out lines, turning the paper sideways to add stanzas, placing wavy marks beside passages he intended to revise. Occasionally he paused to recite a line of verse to Sacristán, who thought Lorca read with "an ardor capable of melting snow." When at last he had completed a draft that satisfied him, Lorca stopped writing.

Drawn from the Old Testament story of Thamar and Amnon, the poem told of a brother who rapes his sister. Because the Gypsies of Andalusia themselves sang the story of Thamar and Amnon, Lorca considered his ballad "Gypsy-Jewish." But his version of the story owed less to the Bible, than to traditional Spanish ballads and to plays by Tirso de Molina and Calderón. In contrast to the straightforward narrative of the Old Testament, Lorca imbued his "Thamar and Amnon" with powerful erotic imagery, relying on metaphor to convey the story's darkest truths:

> *Now he grasps her by the hair,*
> *now he tears her shirt.*
> *Tepid corals sketch*
> *little rivers on a blond map.*

The poem's subject matter betrayed Lorca's growing fascination with sexual instinct. Among those to later praise the work was Salvador Dalí, who told Lorca it was "the best" of his gypsy ballads. The painter especially admired the poem's "chunks of incest."

DALÍ WAS BACK AT THE RESIDENCIA THAT YEAR. In the wake of his expulsion from Madrid's Academy of Fine Arts in 1923, and his subsequent imprisonment in Catalunya, he had shed his timorous ways and embraced the avant-garde with maniacal zeal. He dared others to dispute his passion for the new.

Lorca and fellow residents rallied to Dalí's cause. They proclaimed anything modern good — automobiles, telephones, airplanes, radio. Luis Buñuel bought a gramophone and a stack of American records. Lorca, Dalí and others spent hours in Buñuel's room listening to jazz while sipping rum grog, a drink strictly against house rules. They attended films by such new stars as Buster Keaton, and at the Residencia they practiced their own brand of goofball humor.

Late in the afternoon they would spill into Lorca's room to drink tea, read, talk and smoke. Lorca dubbed these improvised gatherings "meetings of the desperation of tea." The evenings typically lasted until midnight and culminated in a reading from some book. As a rule, Lorca reserved the final passage for himself; when he spotted a line that moved him, he stopped to repeat it. Once, after reading a scene in which a character rolled about on the floor, Lorca and former roommate Pepín Bello suddenly dropped to the floor, laughing, and began to roll around together.

Dozens of pranks, jokes, antics and games evolved. Lorca hosted mass poetry-writing sessions in his room, during which he and his friends invented four-line nonsense poems called "anaglyphs." "Tea, / tea, / hen / and Teotocópuli," read one. Another came up with the idea of a "fart meter": a wooden box with a hole, a candle and a piece of string. Lorca and his friends held private tournaments to see who could expel the most wind. According to Rafael Alberti, who sometimes participated in these competitions, "It took a very strong fart to make the flame swell high enough to light the string."

With Buñuel, Lorca staged innumerable practical jokes. They once coated their faces with rice powder, donned bogus nuns' habits and boarded a city tram, where they cast lascivious glances at their neighbors and rubbed obscenely against male passengers. One drunken evening Buñuel inaugurated the "Order of Toledo," an informal fraternity whose primary purpose was to make inebriated excursions to the city of Toledo, two hours south of Madrid by train. Lorca was among the founding members; Dalí, Bello and Alberti eventually joined the Order. In Toledo, the group's ritual activities included kissing the ground and climbing the cathedral bell tower, then wrapping themselves in bedsheets and wandering the streets, drunk, all night long.

AS PERPETRATORS OF THE OUTLANDISH, Lorca, Buñuel, Dalí and Bello became the nominal leaders of the Residencia avant-garde. Of the four, Bello was often the most ingenious. Buñuel called him a "Surrealist at heart"; Lorca compared him to El Greco. Lifting a phrase from his medical studies, Bello coined the term "putrefaction" to refer to anything outmoded, sacred or anachronistic — anything, in short, that blocked the onset of modernity. He and his friends immediately began using the word as a label for people and things that offended them. Dalí told Bello that at heart "putrefaction" meant "EMOTION. And therefore it's inseparable from human nature." In Dalí's hierarchy, the Pope was a "putrefaction"; so was the current Spanish king, the artist Henri Rousseau and a whole raft of critics, books, paintings and fashions.

Together with Lorca, Dalí began planning a book of putrefactions, to which Lorca was to contribute prose entries and Dalí illustrations. The artist turned out a number of sketches for the book — whimsical drawings of buffoons reminiscent of the grotesque caricatures Lorca had begun producing two years earlier in Granada. But Lorca reneged on his end of the bargain and never drafted so much as a prologue. To Dalí's annoyance, the project died. Yet the friendship prospered.

The two men roamed Madrid together. They gazed at paintings by Velásquez and Raphael in the Prado and listened to jazz in cafés. At the Residencia they once leaned out of a bedroom window and waved white handkerchiefs to passersby while shouting "Heeeelp! Lost at sea!" Forever low on cash, they schemed for ways to supplement their allowances from home. According to Lorca, who may have been lying (he "lied a lot and with pleasure," recalled Pepín Bello,) he and Dalí once sold a mediocre painting to an unsuspecting couple from South America. The two friends celebrated the deed by hiring a pair of taxis to take them home to the Residencia. As they sat together in the first taxi, puffing on Havana cigars, the second car followed behind, empty. Lorca later explained that the second taxi was a *"taxi de respeto* — a car exclusively hired for the sake of respect." The idea, he added, quickly became a fad among rich young men in Madrid.

BY THE SPRING OF 1925, HE AND DALÍ were near-constant companions. They made several weekend excursions to Toledo, and in March they took a trip to the mountains north of Madrid. Each found in the other a reflection of his own beliefs and ambition and, most of all, talent. There was an element of idolatry to their friendship, of mutual awe, but also, increasingly, of love. They understood each other in ways no one else did or could, and as time wore on, they came to need one another with growing urgency.

That spring Dalí invited Lorca to spend Easter week in Catalunya with his family. Lorca begged his parents to let him make the trip. He outlined the various reasons why he had to go: the distinction and wealth of the Dalí family, the fact that Dalí's sister, Ana María, was "one of those girls who is so beautiful she drives you crazy." Clearly, he thought that his parents might relent if they detected a love interest. Furthermore, the visit would give him time to work on at least two new plays. "You know how the countryside and its silence give me all the ideas I have."

His final and most compelling justification for the trip was financial. He told his parents that the Barcelona Atheneum had asked him to give a reading during his stay in Catalunya and had agreed to pay his travel expenses. Given both the money and prestige he stood to gain from the event, he would be foolish to refuse. He did not mention the fact that the Atheneum invitation came from one of Dalí's friends, nor that he and Dalí had apparently persuaded the friend to issue the offer in order to bolster Lorca's case with his parents. Their scheme worked: Lorca received permission to go to Catalunya.

THE VILLAGE OF CADAQUÉS LIES a hundred miles north of Barcelona, in a rocky cove beside the Mediterranean. Traveling by taxi with Dalí from the nearby town of Figueres, Lorca first glimpsed the town from the hills above it and was struck by the purity of what he saw: a crescent of bright white buildings hugging the sea. He later described the setting as "both eternal and actual, but perfect."

As a boy Dalí had spent summers and holidays here with his family. He loved Cadaqués. The town's angular contours and brilliant Mediterranean light filled his canvases in much the same way that the Granadan *vega* filled Lorca's poems. Lorca instinctively understood Dalí's attachment to the place, and within days of his arrival he too felt as though he were treading on sacred ground when he walked among the olive trees that skirted the tiny village.

More than anything it was the warmth of the welcome he received from the Dalí family that made Lorca fall in love with Cadaqués. He and Salvador arrived in time for lunch and immediately sat down at the table with Dalí's father, stepmother and sister. "My friend Federico, whom I've told you about," Dalí announced. By dessert Lorca was on such good terms with the family that it seemed to seventeen-year-old Ana María Dalí "as if we had always known one another."

To his astonishment, Lorca learned that Dalí's father, Salvador Dalí Cusí, a stout, cigar-smoking lawyer, knew a number of his poems by heart. Lorca was even more astonished by Dalí's sister, Ana María, whom he pronounced "without doubt, the most beautiful girl I have seen in my life." Her long, dark hair fell to her shoulders in such a cascade of curls that he was reminded of the angel Gabriel. She had a cherubic face, limpid brown eyes and a soft, coquettish smile. There was both a girlishness to her and a budding sensuality to which Lorca was not immune. One day, as he watched her nap in the sun, he turned to Dalí and exclaimed, "What pretty breasts Ana María has!"

Dalí grabbed Lorca's hands. "Well, touch them, man. Touch them!" he teased.

Dalí himself was entranced by his sister's beauty and repeatedly asked her to pose for him. Eventually this phase of his career became known by Ana María's presence in his canvases. She spent hours standing patiently beside windows in Cadaqués and Figueres, studying the landscape while her brother painted her. They were unusually close — a situation owing to their mother's death four years earlier, when Dalí was nearly seventeen and Ana María twelve. At the time they had turned to one another in grief and bewilderment, and now, four years later, at twenty-two and seventeen, they continued to dote on each other. They played infantile games together, as if by doing so they could somehow recreate the childhood they had so abruptly lost to death. Ana María had a teddy bear named "Little Bear," which she dressed in play clothes and carried with her wherever she went. When she, her brother and Lorca were together in a room, the bear often sat near them on a chair. Dalí sometimes placed a philosophy book between its paws "so that it can learn," he said. He and Lorca adopted the bear as a mascot, and long after leaving Cadaqués Lorca sent messages to the animal. "Give plenty of kisses to the little bear," he once instructed Ana María. "Four days ago I found him smoking a cigar."

In Cadaqués, Lorca behaved as childishly as the two Dalí siblings. He and Salvador had their photograph taken wearing white beach robes and top hats, and posing rakishly beside a table where Ana María stood with a watering can, pretending to sprinkle them. Like a small boy, Lorca frequently taunted his friends. Pouting, he would cry, "You don't love me! Well, then, I'm going away!" He would run off and hide until Dalí and Ana María dutifully began hunting for him, at which point Lorca would reappear, giggling. He drew immense pleasure from these episodes, Ana María remembered, "because then he felt loved."

A T THE SAME TIME HE FELL PREY to sudden and frequent bouts of gloom. His smile would vanish, and a hard, expressionless look grip his face. Both Ana María and her brother were startled by Lorca's brusque mood changes and by his apparent obsession with death. At the Residencia, Dalí had often heard Lorca refer to his own death — sometimes more than once in a given day. On a number of occasions the painter witnessed a bizarre ritual in which Lorca imagined himself dead.

The rite always began late at night, with Lorca calling out to a group of friends, "Hey everyone, this is how I'll look when I die!" He would then throw himself across the bed, feign rigor mortis and direct his companions in a boisterous enactment of his funeral procession through the streets of Granada. The performance invariably ended with Lorca's burial. Afterward he would leap up, laughing, and herd his friends through the door so that he could sleep in peace. Death thus became a familiar presence in his life, an event to be viewed with calm, or even laughter, to be milked for inspiration.

In Cadaqués, Lorca once stretched out on the floor in Dalí's studio and closed his eyes in a death pose. Ana María took his picture while her brother sketched him. Later that year Dalí incorporated Lorca's lifeless face into his painting *Honey Is Sweeter than Blood*.

Both men worked during the Easter holiday. Lorca began a new play, *The Sacrifice of Iphigenia*. Dalí painted from sunrise to dusk in his cluttered gray studio. As he worked, the artist sang to himself through closed lips. To Lorca, the sound resembled "a hive of golden bees." He loved to watch his slender young friend at work.

At night, he and the two Dalís took walks through Cadaqués. Ever in search of new details for his paintings, Dalí scrutinized the light, clouds and sea. Lorca talked of the work he had done that day and later, as moonlight danced across the Mediterranean, recited his poems. His voice mingled with the sound of waves lapping against fishing boats. It was then, recalled Ana María, that the poet entered "his element" and became "perfectly elegant." His husky voice softened into a thing of beauty. "Everything around him was transformed." Language had purified him.

In Cadaqués, as elsewhere, Lorca craved the limelight. In addition to reciting poetry he read his new three-act play about

Mariana Pineda to the Dalí family one afternoon as they sat around the dining room table. He had finished a draft of the work in January. Ana María was so moved by the drama that she wept. Her father let out a triumphant cry and proclaimed Lorca the greatest poet of the century. From that moment on, the plump attorney treated Lorca like a second son.

At the end of Easter week the Dalí family returned to their winter home in Figueres, where Dalí's father arranged for Lorca to give a second reading of *Mariana Pineda* before a group of his friends; they included the editor of one of Barcelona's daily newspapers. Lorca was grateful for the chance to read his drama before such a distinguished audience. To his parents he described the crowd as "the cream of the progressive and intellectual set of Figueres."

HE RETURNED HOME TO GRANADA IN JUNE. He missed Catalunya desperately and sent letters to both Salvador and Ana María Dalí, urging them to visit him. Neither came. Dalí insisted that he could not leave his work.

With Ana María, then seventeen, Lorca struck up a flirtatious correspondence. "I have a portfolio of memories of you and of your laughter that is unforgettable," he confessed to her soon after leaving Catalunya. He remarked on her sun-burnished beauty and called her a "little daughter of the olive trees and niece of the sea!"

But his true passion was for Ana María's brother. Within weeks of his visit to Cadaqués, Lorca began drafting an "Ode to Salvador Dalí," in which he revealed his affection for the painter:

> *I sing a common belief*
> *that unites us in the dark and golden hours.*
> *It is not Art, this light that blinds our eyes.*
> *It is first love, friendship, or fencing.*

As he worked on the ode, Lorca sent passages of the poem to

Dalí, who praised its brilliance and begged to see more. "AH, MY ODE!" he scrawled exuberantly across the top of a letter hailing Lorca as "the only genius of our time." He signed the document, "Dalí Salvador, painter of certain talent and friend (close) of a great POET who is VERY handsome. Goodbye. Oh, your recently shaved face. WET! Your shoehorn, your SUITCASE . . .! Your socks."

Already the two shared a private vocabulary that soon evolved into an encoded language all but indecipherable to outsiders. Week after week letters went back and forth between Catalunya and Granada, and later Madrid. "What are you doing? Are you working?" Dalí asked Lorca in November 1925. "Don't fail to write to me — you, the only interesting man I've ever known." He referred to himself repeatedly as Lorca's "little son" and sent him drawings, collages, photographs, postcards and even a florid Valentine — the essence of putrefaction — stamped "My Beloved Darling."

By January 1926, Lorca could boast to Melchor Fernández Almagro that he enjoyed "an abundant correspondence [with] my friend and inseparable companion Salvador Dalí." Elsewhere he spoke reverently of "the ineffable Dalí." He had not been so intoxicated by another human being since adolescence, when he had pined after María Luisa Egea. She had spurned his love; Dalí did not.

TO LORCA, THE PAINTER'S EXTRAVAGANT, adoring letters were a godsend. But Lorca wanted more. In the summer of 1925, in the weeks following his visit to Cadaqués, he talked anxiously of his desire to see Dalí, and in letters to their mutual friend Benjamín Palencia, a painter, he hinted at the depth of his attachment to "Salvadorcito." Through Palencia, Dalí had promised to send him a pair of his paintings. "They will live in my house and next to my heart," Lorca said.

To admit to himself that he loved Dalí as much as he did was to confront matters Lorca had long sought to suppress. It was a troubling summer. Frustrated by his stalled theatrical career, and increasingly mesmerized by Dalí's radical ideas, he questioned the direction of his work. At home, his parents had once more begun complaining about his apparent unwillingness to make something of himself. Lorca mourned his absent friends. Each evening at dusk he watched the sun cast its golden light across the *vega*. He saw birds glisten like bits of metal in the sky, and he felt as though he had died. "I'm going through one of the toughest crises I've ever experienced," he told Palencia. "Both my literary and emotional work are failing me. I don't believe in anyone. I don't like anyone. I dream of constant dawn, as cold as a spikenard, full of cold smells and exact emotions. An exact tenderness and a hard, intelligent light. We'll see how I escape!"

*L*ORCA KNEW THE PERILS OF HOMOSEXUAL LOVE. He knew about Oscar Wilde's imprisonment, and he had read *De Profundis;* his copy of Wilde's book was heavily marked. He could scarcely have been ignorant of his own country's attitude toward same-sex love. The Arabs who settled Andalusia had once sanctioned it. But the Inquisition had persecuted homosexuals, and the Catholic Church continued to regard them as deviants of the worst sort. Lorca knew how people gossiped; as a teenager he had been ridiculed for his peculiar dress and effeminate ways. At twenty-one he had gone weeping to a friend's house after learning that someone was spreading a rumor that he, Lorca, was homosexual.

For years he had tried to convince both himself and his friends that he was "normal." Although he lacked his brother's polish with women, he made a show of desiring. While vaca-

tioning with his family in Málaga in 1918, he had complained to
an acquaintance, "The hotel is lively but there are no girls." In
truth, Lorca was intimidated by the notion of physical intimacy
with women. His closest friends and confidants had almost
always been men. He loved the frank badinage of the all-male
tertulia, the high jinks of masculine camaraderie at the Residencia.
His poetry revealed his growing fascination with the beauty of
the male form.

He would later admit that since boyhood an "impassioned
force" had driven him toward men, not women. He claimed to
have idolized a particular village boy during his childhood, a
younger neighbor whose friendship Lorca sought to monopolize.
"I wanted him to play only with me." Decades later Lorca still
remembered that early love with an acute sense of joy as well as
privation. "When I eventually realized my preference," he recalled,
"I came to understand that what I liked others thought perverse."

He learned to veil the truth, to flaunt a socially acceptable
facade. Even in the summer of 1925, in the midst of his tur-
bulent awakening to a new emotional, sexual and aesthetic self,
he understood intuitively that he must dissemble. To his lifelong
friend Melchor Fernández Almagro he said only, "I'm getting into
problems I should have addressed long ago." Newly consumed by
the notion of masquerade, he began sketching clowns and harle-
quins whose sad faces belied the merriment of their dress.

He turned to metaphor as a means of both veiling and articu-
lating the truth. To Ana María Dalí he confessed that he'd had a
difficult summer and longed to be near the sea. More than ever,
landlocked Granada epitomized his repressed desires, and the
sea his longing for emotional and sexual freedom. "The young
ladies of Granada go up to their whitewashed terraces to see the
mountains and *not* see the ocean," he wrote delicately to Dalí's
sister. "In the afternoon they dress in gauze and vaporous satiny

things and go down to the promenade where the fountains flow like diamonds and there is an old anguish of roses and amorous melancholy....The young ladies of Granada have no love for the sea. They have enormous nacar shells with painted sailors and that is the way they see it; and great conch shells in their salons, and that is the way they hear it." A trip to Málaga with his family towards the end of the summer "saved" his life. There, as in Cadaqués, Lorca basked in the life-giving force of the Mediterranean. The moment one reaches Málaga, he told Benjamín Palencia, "Dionysus rubs your head with his sacred horns and your soul turns the color of wine."

BY LATE SEPTEMBER, HE HAD BEGUN WRITING what he called "erotic poetry." The effort invigorated him. He wrote eight poems in all, each a brief, ironic work depicting a particular woman and the sexual trait by which she is known. The poems suggest Lorca's deepening aversion to the female anatomy. He describes the breasts of a spinster as "black melons." Of another woman he writes, "Beneath the moon-dark rosebay / you looked ugly naked." In the short poem "Lucía Martínez" he assumes the voice of a predatory Don Juan:

> *Here I am, Lucía Martínez.*
> *I've come to devour your mouth*
> *and drag you off by the hair*
> *into the seashells of daybreak.*

> *Because I want to and I can.*

The poems were a departure for Lorca, his first foray into what he called "a distinguished field." They made him feel young again. "Am I backward?" he asked Fernández Almagro. "What is this? It seems as though I've only just come into my youth. That's why when I'm sixty I won't be old....I'm never going to be *old*."

Age frightened him nearly as much as heterosexual sex. Both were the subject of a new play he began that summer, *The Love of Don Perlimplín with Belisa in his Garden*, the story of a marriage between an elderly man and a beautiful young woman whose seductive appearance on their wedding night so intimidates her husband that he is unable to consummate their marriage. Lorca subtitled the work an "Erotic *Aleluya*" — a reference to the popular Spanish broadsheets, or *aleluyas*, printed with colorful vignettes of stock characters, he and his brother had read as children. Again Lorca was mixing genres. The plot of *Perlimplín* enabled him both to revisit an art form he had loved in boyhood, and to explore a favorite and familiar theme, the conflict between spiritual and sensual love. Perhaps for that reason the play flowed quickly from his pen. Lorca finished a first draft by January 1926.

He remained restless. In the midst of his work on *Perlimplín* he began writing a series of short, highly experimental dialogues. "Pure poetry. Naked," he said of them. Terse and unorthodox, the miniature works sketched an amusing portrait of the life Lorca had known the previous year in Madrid with Dalí and their friends. He titled one work "Dialogue of the Residencia." Others included "Dialogue with Luis Buñuel," a conversation over tea at the Residencia; "Buster Keaton's Stroll," a short homage to Keaton and the silent films Lorca had grown to love; and "Mute Dialogue of the Carthusians," a wordless conversation — expressed principally through punctuation marks — between two Carthusian monks. Dalí's presence in the dialogues, explicit as well as implicit, was pervasive. On the manuscript of "Buster Keaton's Stroll," Lorca wrote, "Goodbye Dalilaitita / Daliminita / Dalipiruta / Damitira / Demeter / Dalí." And then: "Write to me at once. / At once. / At once. At once."

1926-27

Dalí's fame, like Lorca's, was growing. In late 1925 he had held his first painting exhibition in Barcelona, at the prestigious Dalmau Galleries. A critical as well as commercial triumph, the show caught the eye of Pablo Picasso. When Dalí visited Paris, the two artists spent several hours together in Picasso's studio. During his stay in Madrid that spring Dalí provoked another of his short-lived scandals. Having re-enrolled in Madrid's Academy of Fine Arts after his expulsion in 1923, he showed up at the school in mid-June 1926 for a final examination. Dressed in a checked coat with a gardenia in its lapel, and bolstered by a glass of absinthe, he curtly told his examiners, "Given that none of the professors at the school . . . has the competence to judge me, I withdraw." For the second time in his life, he was expelled from the institution. Dalí went home to Catalunya, intent on persuading his father to send him to Paris. He believed that in France he would "definitively seize power!"

Lorca continued to idolize him. Each viewed the other as his most discerning audience. After his Barcelona exhibition, Dalí sent Lorca press clippings from the show, but only "the harshest criticism." The other reviews, he explained, were of no interest "because they are so unconditionally enthusiastic." In March 1926, Dalí confessed to Lorca that he had spent the whole of one Sunday afternoon rereading Lorca's letters to him. "Little son! They're extraordinary. In each line there are suggestions for numerous books, theatrical works, paintings, etc., etc., etc., etc." A week or so later he sent another note. "Do you love me?" he asked.

He still wanted Lorca to collaborate with him on a book of putrefactions, and they discussed the project during Dalí's visit to Madrid that spring. But Lorca had more pressing matters to address — chiefly the business of finding a producer for *Mariana*

Pineda. He told his parents he intended to remain in Madrid until he had resolved the issue. After Dalí's departure, Lorca lingered in the capital, but without results. Eduardo Marquina could not find a producer for the play, and no one else to whom Lorca showed the script was willing to take on the work. Lorca blamed the theater establishment. "This business of dealing with impresarios is one of the most repugnant things in the world, because they're all a bunch of idiots," he complained to his parents. "The Spanish theater is in the hands of the worst riffraff, actors as well as playwrights."

AFTER A COUPLE OF MONTHS IN MADRID, Lorca left the capital empty-handed and went home to Granada for the summer. He invited Dalí to join him, but the painter declined, citing the need to prepare for his next exhibition. Unlike Lorca, who yearned for Dalí's physical presence, the artist was content with a mostly cerebral friendship. He needed Lorca imaginatively, not physically. At least four canvases in Dalí's upcoming exhibition bore hints of Lorca's heart-shaped face.

In their letters the two began to make cryptic, homoerotic references to Saint Sebastian, by coincidence the patron of Cadaqués. Dalí referred to Sebastian's "delicious" agony and, invoking another shared icon, the fish, invited Lorca to embrace "my new type of Saint Sebastian, consisting of the pure transmutation of the Arrow of the Sole." Both men viewed the figure of Sebastian as a provocative one, at once inviting and impassive, a perfect emblem of the emotional control each now sought to achieve in his work. Dalí called Sebastian "Saint Objectivity." In a letter to Jorge Guillén, Lorca defined true poetry as "love, effort and *renunciation.* (Saint Sebastian)."

More so than Dalí, Lorca struggled to find a balance between his old work and his new. He continued to be inspired by Andalusia, even as he looked to Catalunya and to France for enlightenment. But it was a constant battle. While on holiday in the *vega* with his family that summer, he told his brother he was sick of the village of Asquerosa and its petty inhabitants. "In the country one seeks innocence," he grumbled, adding drolly, "I attribute all this to the fact that there are no cows here, and no grazing of any sort."

LANGUAGE ALLOWED LORCA TO DO ON PAPER what he longed to do in life: prevaricate. *Songs* is filled with terms such as "mute," "echo," "shadow" and "mirror" — words that enabled Lorca to stress the layered nature of truth. Throughout the collection surfaces mislead, shadows contradict and personality is mutable. "I used to be. / I once was. / But I am not," confides the narrator of "Monday, Wednesday, and Friday." (While at work on the collection, Lorca admitted to Melchor Fernández Almagro that in "everything" he found "a painful absence of my *own* and true person.")

Lorca's interest in concealment sprang partly from his growing need to suppress certain aspects of himself. In *Songs* he hints at his ambivalent feelings toward love and sex. His evocations of heterosexual love are occasionally tinged with a sense of regret:

> *The girl goes through my brow.*
> *Oh, what ancient feeling!*
>
> . . .
>
> *Full moon brunette.*
> *What do you want of my desire?*

The collection includes the series of "erotic poems" Lorca wrote in 1925 in the wake of his first, impassioned visit to Dalí in Cadaqués, poems that exude a triumphant — if ironic — male sexuality. In "Song of the Fairy," part of another series called "Games," Lorca writes with amusement of a "fairy" homosexual in a silk dressing gown who "arranges / the curls on his head" while the neighbors watch from their windows and smile. The brief, unorthodox work suggests both a certain discomfort with same-sex love and an attraction to it:

> *Scandal was shuddering,*
> *streaked like a zebra.*
> *The fairies of the south*
> *sing on roof terraces.*

In a complex series of six poems entitled "Three Portraits with Shadow," Lorca intimates his unease with the female sex ("No one would love you like me / if you'd only change my heart!") and seems to embrace love of the self, or those like the self. True to the overall concept of the book, it is only in the so-called "shadow" poems — "Bacchus," "Venus" and "Narcissus," each of which appears in smaller type after its "portrait," respectively, of Verlaine, Juan Ramón Jiménez and Debussy — that Lorca ventures to signal the truth, and then he does so obliquely, relying on metaphor to convey what he cannot speak. "Boy! / You'll fall into the river," he warns in "Narcissus." "Deep down there's a rose / with another river inside."

As in all of Lorca's work, there is an undertow of loss and sorrow in *Songs*, and a sometimes acute consciousness of human mortality, but despite the collection's occasional sobriety, it is the most buoyant volume of poetry Lorca was to create. Individual poems have titles like "Silly Song," "Useless Song," "Sung Song." Many are dedicated to Lorca's friends at the Residencia (one inscription reads: "to Luis Buñuel's head. En gros plan"), and the collection as a whole is marked by the sort of high-spirited fun that characterized life at the Madrid institution.

In shaping the book, Lorca had sifted through almost six years' worth of poems, many of which he had originally written for other collections, chiefly *Suites* and *Poem of the Deep Song*.

As a consequence he had also had to rethink each of those books. The process caused him "genuine anguish," he said. But in the end he was pleased with the results. "The songs remain girded to my body and I am master of the book," he told Jorge Guillén. "A bad poet . . . very well! But master of my bad poetry!"

Any doubts he had about the collection were groundless. *Songs* was Lorca's first definitive book, a leap forward in the evolution of his style, and while it received scant critical notice at the time, those who did review it were struck by its originality. *El Sol*'s Ricardo Baeza praised *Songs* as "a poetry of codes and arabesques." Luis Montanyá, writing in the avant-garde Catalan journal *L'Amic de les Arts*, called *Songs* "pure poetry . . . an authentic book of poems." Enrique Díez-Canedo, the Madrid correspondent for Argentina's *La Nación*, extolled Lorca's "penetrating poetic vision."

Dalí voiced his qualified approval of the book. Although he claimed to prefer the poetry of "a nickle-plated motor" to that of an old Granadan song, he nevertheless admired Lorca's "delightful songs." Yet he could not refrain from noting that Lorca's lyrical vision of a timeless Andalusia no longer suited a world that had just seen Lindbergh cross the Atlantic. "Your songs are Granada without trams, without even airplanes," Dalí wrote. He conceded, however, that Lorca would go on doing whatever he wished. "That much we already know."

1927

At twenty-three, Dalí was on the brink of international fame. In late 1926 he held his second painting exhibition in Barcelona. The show drew buyers from Paris and a representative from Pittsburgh's Carnegie Institute, who purchased two Dalí canvases.

In February 1927 the Spanish army drafted the artist for nine months of military service. "*Carísimo amigo*," Dalí wrote to Lorca in March. "You can't imagine. I've been a soldier for one month!" Being in the army was a lark. "I'm strong from boxing and very suntanned," he reported in May. He also missed Lorca: "Now we're beginning to need our madnesses, our wanderings about, our tears and our laughter, and our hunger!"

Nearly a year had passed since their last rendezvous in Madrid. With *Mariana Pineda* slated to open that summer in Barcelona, they expected to see each other soon. In late March Lorca went to Madrid to meet with Margarita Xirgu to finalize plans for the production. From there he intended to go to Barcelona to begin rehearsals. He told Pepín Bello it was the start of a new era for him: "I'm saying goodbye to Segovia and Toledo. That's how it must be. I dream of Paris and another more enjoyable life."

But he needed money for the trip, and his father, exasperated with Lorca's spending habits, hesitated to give it. His parents were especially put out with him because during his brief stay in Madrid in March he had squandered a large amount of money. He claimed it wasn't his fault. Upon his arrival the Residencia had been full, he explained, and he had been forced to eat in cafés and stay in a costly hotel (the cheaper places were too far away to accommodate his "theater life"). He had also found it necessary to send a bouquet of roses to Xirgu and to host a banquet for several journalist friends in order to persuade them to go to Barcelona later in the season to review *Mariana*. "The money disappears like water," he said. "I'm not a spendthrift."

His father viewed matters differently. For years he had indulged Lorca financially. A two-month allowance sometimes vanished in three days — spent on little more than outings with friends. In letters home, Lorca invariably asked for money, time and again insisting that his expenses were "necessary." His request could be blunt: "Send me fifty pesetas in your next letter. I need it." Usually his parents obliged him. They sent money so that he could buy food, shoes, hats, a new winter coat. "You know that we want you to be decently dressed and not to have to beg things from people," his mother wrote.

But in the spring of 1927 his father balked, and threatened to withhold funds for Lorca's trip to Barcelona. Lorca was devastated. In a six-page letter defending himself and his goals — yet another plea for potential respect — he promised his father that he would "more than repay" the expense of the trip once he had collected his earnings from *Mariana*. Why begrudge him the money he so desperately needed — especially now, when he had just spent ten months in Granada "with three-and-a-half pesetas to my name. (So to speak.)"? If his parents refused to pay his way, he would simply go back to Granada and stay there. Xirgu could produce *Mariana* "any way she likes, and with the scenery and the acting as she sees fit," Lorca sulked. "Anything to keep from upsetting you."

Worn down from years of argument, and newly reminded of his son's unyielding determination, his father relented. By mid-May, Lorca was on his way to Barcelona.

*I*N HIS SOLDIER'S UNIFORM, DALÍ LOOKED as dashing as a Hollywood star. Tall, suntanned, slim, he posed cooly beside Lorca not long after Federico reached Barcelona that spring, and the two had their picture taken. Dalí wore his hair slicked back from his porcelain face; he placed his hands comfortably in his pockets and extended one uniformed leg gracefully in front of the other. Beside him Lorca seemed young and unrefined. He wore a rumpled gray suit and held his hands stiffly together in front of him. An acquaintance who met him during his visit to Catalunya in 1927 recalled that he "exuded 'south' from every pore." Powerless to match Dalí's urban polish, Lorca traded on his rustic Andalusian roots. He cheerfully mocked the ardent Catalan nationalism then rampant in Barcelona, telling one local reporter, "I'm from the Kingdom of Granada!" He began wearing a red carnation in his lapel.

Throughout the two-month rehearsal period for *Mariana Pineda*, Lorca shuttled back and forth between the Dalí home in nearby Figueres and a hotel room in Barcelona, which he and Dalí sometimes shared when Dalí was able to get leave from the army. The two friends wandered the city together, lost in passionate conversation about art and aesthetics, or about Lorca's play, which Dalí had agreed to design. Lorca deluged the painter with sketches and photographs of typical Andalusian settings. He praised Dalí's "shrewdly intuited" take on the play's design, while Dalí, in turn, gamely applauded Lorca's "sophisticated sentimentality."

FEWER THAN TWENTY-FOUR HOURS after the premiere of his *Mariana Pineda*, Lorca opened an exhibition of his drawings in Barcelona's celebrated Dalmau Galleries, the city's leading proponent of avant-garde art. With the exception of two private showings of his sketches at a friend's home in Granada, where the drawings were hung from curtains with pins, he had never publicly shown his work before. Mostly he sketched for pleasure, using whatever was handy — a piece of stationery, a crayon, his sister's colored pencils. He had no desire to be a painter, he joked, because his parents could not tolerate stains in the house. But Dalí admired his visual intuition (which he described as "aphrodisiac") and together with several other Barcelona friends persuaded the diminutive, white-haired Josep Dalmau to present an exhibition of Lorca's work in his gallery.

Dalmau had long championed the avant-garde. He had introduced Barcelona audiences to the work of Filippo Marinetti and Marcel Duchamp, and he had helped launch the careers of Juan Gris, Joan Miró and Pablo Picasso. Dalí had twice shown his paintings in Dalmau's galleries, and he owed his success in part to the visibility those exhibitions had given him. Lorca's week-long exhibit drew less attention than Dalí's, but it did receive a few flattering reviews from friends, including Dalí, and to Lorca's astonishment he sold four drawings. He gave the rest away to his Catalan friends.

An eclectic mix of old and new, traditional and avant-garde, the drawings in the exhibition complemented Lorca's poetry collection *Songs*, published one month earlier. Both demonstrated his abiding love of popular Andalusian motifs, his newfound admiration for cubism, and his increasing preoccupation with identity. In a number of his Dalmau sketches Lorca superimposed one dreamlike face on another, as if to offer a graphic interpretation of the ideas he had explored in *Songs*: "Woodcutter./ Sever me from my shadow." Years later he described one of his double-faced images as a self-portrait that shows "man's capacity for crying as well as winning." The works encapsulate the split personal conviction that without sorrow, joy was inconceivable, without death, life incomprehensible.

In a somber drawing called "The Kiss," he sketched a face much like his own, with dense black eyebrows and a wedge of black hair, joined at the lips to a second, featureless face whose oval contour resembles Dalí's. In his own work Dalí too had recently begun pairing Lorca's face with his. Each man appeared to covet, or fear, losing himself in the other. Aesthetically they had never been closer. Dalí said later that during this phase of his career, "for the duration of an eclipse," Lorca's shadow "came to darken the virginal originality of my spirit and of my flesh."

Lorca was equally swayed by Dalí. His Barcelona drawings revealed the degree to which he had absorbed the painter's cubist aesthetic and shared Dalí's enthusiasm for Surrealism. The exhibition included a formal portrait of Dalí, one of several Lorca made during this period. He had developed his own icon for the artist's face: a Modigliani-like ovoid with almond-shaped eyes, black eyebrows and full lips. In one of Lorca's portraits of the artist, Dalí appears as a kind of fecund priest wearing a bishop's miter, with fish nibbling at each of the fingers on his right hand. Rife with Freudian overtones, this intensely private work referred to a world only Lorca and Dalí fully understood. Lorca gave the drawing to the painter, who kept it for decades. By way of explaining the image, Dalí said only, "Lorca saw me as an incarnation of life, graced like a dark god."

DAYS AFTER THE CLOSING of both *Mariana Pineda* and his Dalmau exhibition, Lorca boarded a bus with Salvador and Ana María Dalí, and the three took off for Cadaqués. They sat side by side on a rooftop bench. The instant Lorca caught his first glimpse of the village in the distance, he shrieked: "Cadaquéééés! Cadaquéééés!" The Dalís quickly chimed in.

At nineteen, Ana María was leaner and more graceful than she had been during Lorca's first visit to the town, in 1925. Her long, angelic curls were gone, replaced by a stylish 1920s bob. Lorca adored her. At dusk the two took walks together, ambling hand in hand through groves of olive trees while church bells pealed and the sun sank beneath the mountains, casting its pink light on the small white town. Lorca often wore a fisherman's shirt Ana María had made for him. Asked years afterward whether Lorca had been in love with her, Ana María merely blushed. That he loved her was certain — but in ways neither seemed able to articulate.

On Sundays the two attended Mass together. Dalí refused to join them. "I've seen it before," he quipped. But Lorca found the ritual soothing. As he stood beside Ana María in the small sanctuary, immersed in gestures and phrases he had known since boyhood, he seemed "in ecstasy." He continued to identify not with the authoritarian Father of Old Testament doctrine, but with the New Testament Christ: symbol of goodness and love, proof that human charity might transcend evil and offset the capriciousness of fate. Only in church, thought Ana María, was Lorca unafraid of death. Elsewhere it obsessed him. Like a frightened child, he insisted on taking their hands whenever he went for a walk with the two Dalís. "He was afraid of dying," Ana María believed, "and it seemed to him that by holding our hands he could remain anchored to life." At the beach he swam only in shallow water, and even then he clung to Ana María's hand. When she and Dalí ventured farther out to the sea, Lorca remained on shore. He was terrified of drowning.

Even small things alarmed him. At the slightest hint of a sore throat, he insisted that Ana María take his temperature and prepare inhalations of eucalyptus leaves. Because they loved him they indulged him. (Later, Lorca apologized to Ana María for his "grave throat illness, which caused you so much trouble.") The three spent whole days playing games together. Dalí and Lorca took turns pretending to be a capricious child, a *"babouet,"* who refused to walk or eat. When Lorca played the *babouet* he demanded to be told terrifying stories with unexpectedly comforting endings.

They went sailing together, took part in local festivals, played records all day long, and at night, with the guitarist Regino Saínz — who was visiting Cadaqués — sat on the beach, while Lorca sang folk songs or recited poems. In dozens of artfully arranged photographs they immortalized their fun: Ana María, holding a phonograph and a stack of records on her lap; Dalí standing alone in a white terry cloth robe, bronzed and sultry, his hair damp from the sea; Lorca, clowning on the beach in bathing trunks and a robe, his chunky legs draped in a showgirl's pose, an impish grin on his face. In one snapshot he and Dalí sat across from each other at a table with Lorca's bathrobe cord stretched between their foreheads, as though they were transmitting thoughts back and forth. In another picture, each displayed an emblem of his artistic temperament. Dalí, who fancied himself a rational Apollonian, held a triangle, while Lorca, his hair slicked back, one hand resting on Salvador's knee, clasped a wine glass.

Lorca's stay in Cadaqués, though brief, was rapturous. He subsequently told a friend that Dalí inspired in him "the same pure emotion" he felt in the presence of the baby Jesus, "abandoned in the Portico of Bethlehem, with the whole germ of the crucifixion already latent beneath the straws of the cradle." Incapable of resisting the painter, he helped Dalí draft and sign a strident "Anti-Artistic Manifesto" exalting the machine age and condemning much of the very literature and art Lorca had once admired. Other friends were alarmed by Dalí's increasingly rigid views on art and his newly "materialistic, irreligious and objective" behavior. But Lorca maintained that nothing was more dramatic than Dalí's objectivity, and he allowed himself to be swept up in the painter's escalating quest for radical new images and ideas — one of which, paradoxically, was Saint Sebastian, who became for Dalí a paradigm of the emotional control he sought.

The martyred saint had been an intimate point of contact between the two friends for at least a year. In March 1927, Dalí signed a letter to Lorca, "Your Saint Sebastian." Even Ana María was in on the secret. On the back of a postcard to Lorca she wrote, "I'm sending you this card because you might like it; but don't show it to Saint Sebastian. It would be improper." Both men were intrigued by the iconography of the saint: his manly beauty and his passive, at times ecstatic response to the arrows piercing his flesh. Lorca came to believe that "one of man's most beautiful postures is that of Saint Sebastian." He meant the posture of defeat, willingly accepted.

Dalí persisted in calling Sebastian "Saint Objectivity." In late July he published an exhaustive prose poem on the martyr in the Catalan journal *L'Amic de les Arts*. Dedicated "To F. García Lorca," Dalí's meandering poem extols Sebastian as an exemplar of the modern age. In Sebastian's pose of "exquisite agony," the saint embodies an aesthetic of objectivity that offers a foil to the sentimentality and "putrefaction" Dalí despised. On a more personal level, Sebastian reminded the painter of Lorca. He told Lorca that while at work on the poem, it had often seemed to him that the saint "is you....We'll see if Saint Sebastian turns out to be you."

Through the image of Sebastian the two made sly allusions to the intense emotional — and conceivably physical — nature of their involvement. Dalí spoke bluntly of the saint's "*unwounded ass.*" Lorca was more oblique. "Saint Sebastian's arrows are made of steel," he wrote to Dalí later that summer, "but the difference between you and me is that you see them as firmly fixed and robust, short arrows that don't come undone, and I see them as long...at the moment of the wound. Your Saint Sebastian of ivory contrasts with mine of flesh who is dying all the time, and that's how it must be."

*T*O WHAT DEGREE THE MARTYR REFLECTED Lorca's private relationship with the artist remains unclear. Years later Dalí claimed to have spurned Lorca's sexual advances. But

others who knew the artist — Pepín Bello, Luis Buñuel, Rafael
Martínez Nadal — suspected Dalí of distorting the truth in
order to shock or amuse his admirers, much as he had once
feigned love for an adolescent girl because he enjoyed deluding
her. Bello and Buñuel both believed Dalí was "asexual," a chaste
Apollo to Lorca's earthbound Dionysus.

Dalí's paintings imply otherwise. By 1927 he had replaced
the neoclassical lines of his earlier canvases with the stark land-
scapes of a Freudian world. His sensual portraits of Ana María
had given way to cryptic representations of Lorca — often
shown as a decapitated head with closed eyes — surroundeed
by jarring manifestations of Dalí's subconscious: nude female
torsos, severed hands, rotting animals, airplanes, fish, phallic
gadgets, genitalia. His ambiguous, at times misogynist depictions
of women, together with the prevalence of both homo- and
autoerotic images, signal the depth of Dalí's sexual malaise and
suggest that in all likelihood he and Lorca engaged in a short-
lived physical affair.

Dalí was obsessed by Lorca, and troubled by his obsession.
In several paintings he layered Lorca's features over his own or
placed one man's face in the other's shadow. At times he simply
fused the two faces. Their lives were similarly intertwined. Dalí
was beginning to write poetry, while Lorca spent more and more
time drawing. In their work, they spoke the same metaphorical
language. Each heaped praise on the other. "Federico is better
than ever," Dalí wrote to Luis Buñuel in Paris that summer.
"He's the great man. His drawings are brilliant."

Buñuel was appalled by the intensity of Dalí's attachment to
Lorca. Perhaps because he resented Lorca's refusal to collaborate
with him on a film the previous year, or more probably because
he detected Lorca's homosexuality and objected to it, Buñuel
had come to loathe what he described as Lorca's "extreme nar-

cissism" and "terrible aestheticism." He told Pepín Bello that unless Dalí escaped to Paris, the painter would amount to nothing. Only in Paris, Buñuel said, could Dalí "remake himself, away from García's ill-fated influence."

CRY WOLF

Ronit Matalon

AUGUST 1998 WAS HARD. TEL AVIV VOMITED ITSELF in your face, expelled you out of itself. Even early morning, which usually allows the city streets some lucidity, was hard. The heavy heat, the humidity, the air saturated with the smoke of buses and the stench of garbage cans — these all congealed, turned into a three-dimensional entity, which crouched upon the city all the way to the seashore, buried the city underneath.

Between six and eight in the evening there came a turn for the worse. The city, after absorbing all day the heat, the pollution, the stifling air, now ejected them mercilessly. It exhaled them rhythmically and monotonously, never reaching a cathartic climax, never finding itself. Everything stood still.

The weather felt like a sign, and this in itself pointed to a sense of desperation. Where there's despair, there appear symbols, language that strives to go beyond immediate meaning, metaphors. But this is not the worse: our marvelous 20th century leads to the death of the image, to a despair which no longer places any hope in language. Something in the totality of the Israeli experience may well annihilate the option of memory, erase the possibility of comparison which memory allows.

Erasing is an important word. I feel that Israeli culture is becoming a culture of perpetual erasure. Compassion is an even more important word. Israeli space is pitiless. In Hebrew, the word for pity or compassion, RAHAMIM, comes from the same root as womb, REHEM. The womb can contain life, protect life until it matures.

Protection is a word at least as important as compassion. What are they protecting, these doglike bronze wolves (or are they wolflike bronze dogs?) in Yaacov Dorchin's sculpture, at the heart of Tel Aviv? Whom are they guarding?

*S*INCE A COFFEE SHOP OPENED in front of this sculpture, I go there often. The coffee shop, the square, the sculpture, occupy one of the busiest intersections in the city. Here all edges of Tel Aviv's urban existence meet for a moment, yearning and corruption blend. The tree-lined boulevard could have directly reached the beach, were it not arbitrarily truncated by a road. The traffic of buses is relentless, soot covers everything, the little stores on King George Street remind one of the wretchedness of the 1950s. Passersby; Russian transients who doze on boulevard benches; beggars who nag the coffee shop customers, while the waiters angrily try to drive them away; dog owners who nonchalantly walk their dogs to the flower bed under the sculpture, waiting for them to use it as their toilet.

Across the intersection, the Dizengoff Center apartment towers rise, the shopping center itself looking wide and roundish,

like the fat body of a laundry woman, too large to be taken in in
a single glance.

There is a sense of abandon and uprootedness about this
space, which resembles a square, yearns to be a square, but still
is not really a square.

D ORCHIN'S SCULPTURE, "A WELL AND FOUR DOGS,"
stands in this fake square and tells a complex story
about being uprooted and abandoned. The story it tells is full of
tensions, contrasts and contradictions. Some people dislike it for
this reason. As for me, it breaks my heart.

I'll try telling the story.

First, there was the container. The large iron container, which
looks like a boiler. In another series of works Dorchin calls it a
"blocked well." It is placed on a strange podium, slightly elevat-
ed, which brings to mind intersecting railroad tracks, anchored
in the simplest, most basic symmetries. A firm, square founda-
tion, invulnerable to the forces of nature, a cross carrying the
huge container: all remnants, ready-mades, remnants mixed with
ready-mades, a drastic restriction of the artist's intervention.

The strict symmetry is kept in the upper part of the container,
which seems to throw things into space, gurgling them out: four
pieces of ploughs facing in four directions, four doglike wolves
watching in four directions. The order is regular: plough, wolf,
plough, wolf, plough, wolf, plough, wolf. The ploughs appear to
stand upside down: they contain the potential mobility of large
pedals, asking to be pressed, moved, activated. This illusion of
potential mobility is critical: these pedals have no direction.
Everything is dismembered, taken apart, fixed anew, frozen still.

Frozen is a key word here. The frozen feeling in Dorchin's
sculpture has a first name, not only a surname. Its first name is
infertility, the barrenness of an object which can no longer fulfill

its function in the world.

This frozen barrenness results from the way these remnants and ready-mades were utilized, taken apart and reassembled. The huge tube, a container turned upside down, contains an allusion to what it once was, to what it could do. Each component of the sculpture, except for the bronze cast wolves, contains simultaneously an allusion to its past and its potential in the world. Once turned on its head, this hidden potential became a promise which will never be realized: the container is doomed to cease being a container, the inverted ploughs are barred from ever being ploughs.

This deflection of the object from its function, this sterilization of potential, conveys cruelty. The discourse on varieties of cruelty in Dorchin's sculpture is no arrogant or self-righteous sermon; it is a wound that makes one shiver, a durable wound that keeps making its presence felt.

Durability is a big issue here. When the two forces, frozenness and durability, face each other, one of the stronger dialogues in this sculpture is created between movement and immobility *and* this specific form of movement.

First and foremost, rust is the enduring liquidating force here. The container is not painted; it is rusty. The power of rust, the movement of rust in and out, overcomes all provocations: every now and then someone scribbles some graffiti or a drawing on the sculpture, and the rust hurries out and swallows it all up, tooth and nail, covers everything with vindictive stubbornness.

There is no glory in the enduring destructive force of rust. It's the durability of the wretched. The same wretched endurance, the acceptance of minimum standards, relinquishing a priori any brittle beauty which may require cultivation, characterizes the sculpture's milieu: it stands on a bed of tough, faceless, resilient plants, almost suffocated by the dog shit.

From above, from the heights of the container, ready to leap, the bronze wolves watch the dogs. There is a process at work in two directions at once: while the rust in the container eats on and on in solitary labor, the bronze wolves are frozen in their movement, laboring with the sun, reacting to the sun.

THE SUN IS THE HEART OF THE SCULPTURE'S DRAMA. It is a sculpture dedicated to the sun, and it refers to the history of the visual arts in Israel, which always put at center stage their relation to the harsh Israeli sun, to the dazzling Israeli light.

Dorchin's version is based on a constant reaction to the sun, to its blinding impact as a prime mover. This container is a well, exposed to the sun. The sun strikes at it incessantly. The sculpture wants to be struck by the sun: it confronts it, unblinking, imprisoning the sun inside itself. It is an impermeable reservoir, all filled with the sun.

The sun alone could tip the balance in the tense relation between the lively and the frozen in the sculpture: the sharp bright light, its variations, the shade — all these implant in us the intense illusion of the bronze wolves as lively, tense, ready to leap. The tension of a split second before the deed, before the catastrophe, before everything falls apart and chaos takes over: the doglike wolves abandoning their passive on-guard position, free to hunt, devour, raise havoc.

But this sculpture, more than speaking of a potential catastrophe, is busy with a catastrophe which already took place. Those bronze wolves at the top tensely await a disaster which has already happened. Or are they themselves the disaster?

There is horror in their anticipation, and something ridiculous, and an inability to tip the balance between the horror and the ridiculous. What the hell are they guarding, what is there in the container to protect?

We don't see the inside, we can't. The inside, the contents, the justification for the bronze wolves' tense anticipation, is a secret which gradually loses its content, becomes more and more insipid the more you contemplate. The sculpture forces us to swallow the commonplace *they guard the territory*, while we cannot see or know what is the content of this territory. What counts is the lookout, which itself becomes the principal content. We can judge it only by the delegates it sends out: wild animals and brutal rules of survival. If you don't stay on your guard, you will be devoured; if you approach, you'll get hit.

THIS IS PART OF THE STORY, BUT NOT ALL OF IT. If Dorchin was through here, in the cruel simplicity of accusations, we could turn our eyes aside, dismiss the whole thing. Angry protests may become a didactic luxury, a privilege claimed at times by certain fashionable forms of political art, justifying in the name of justice a certain utopian terrorism of the correct viewpoint.

But it's the other way around with Dorchin. He put a big stake at the center of the city, and the question what is to be sacrificed on it, who is to be burnt, has no single meaning; it may lead to numerous mutually exclusive answers. This perplexing confusion arouses enormous pain.

How lonely, how pathetic, how helpless, are these bronze wolves, who look — after all — too small. And those inverted ploughs, ready to move, resemble not so much powerful weapons as rather ancient, clumsy frogs; they're a pitiable relic of a bygone civilization.

Dorchin's way of assembling the elements here conveys delicacy and pity. The way the iron becomes personified grants the sculpture a nearly tragic dimension.

The arbitrary, symmetrical assembly; the absurd quality of the bronze wolves; the personification of the iron — all make a statement about a forced, arbitrary strength, not an organic strength.

These clumsy links appear to be Dorchin's complex and intense way of speaking of uprootedness, of the brutal existence which uprootedness may be connected to. This uprootedness is necessarily connected to all manner of arbitrary links, objects divorced from their function, barrenness and infertility, absurdity and horror.

*T*HIS APPEARS TO BE THE STORY Dorchin is telling us about ourselves. It is not an easy story. In mid-August it seems almost impossible, especially as the waiters in the coffee shop in front of the sculpture belong, I suspect, to some sect pledged to demonstrative unpleasantness.

At the table on my right a young mother, cradling a baby in her arms, scolds me about my cigarette. I snuff it out, annoyed — she sits with her infant engulfed by the exhaust fumes of the buses, and is concerned about the cigarette?

Sentences bounce in my head, like the colorful numbered balls in a big glass bubble in the lottery. Look honey, I tell her, this is not America, it's the Third World. In the Third World, people smoke, and keep smoking, because they know they cannot beat death. In America they think they will never die, they play tricks on death. When I smoked in New York — only in the streets, of course — I changed class, I declared myself a new class. I joined the blacks, the Puerto Ricans, the homeless who asked me for a cigarette, with whom I was happy to share. There, it's all classes. Here, there is still something left of the "people." Maybe that is the last remnant of the fantasy of a people: executives and laborers, rich and poor, they all smoke.

The coffee shop tables in the street start retreating to the meager shadow under the umbrella. The air is pierced by the siren of a police car, or maybe an ambulance. Two motorcycles climb on the pavement near the coffee shop, alarming the drunk who fell asleep on the bench by the sculpture. The paving stones in this expansive, shaded space are broken and tilted, full of cracks and bulges. You only discover that when you step on them, not from afar.

There is a rare generosity in this square, in the softness of the old olive trees. A precious, relaxed moment in the history of this Mediterranean city is enfolded here, a unique moment in which the civic and urban thoughts of city builders, rather than the greed of developers, set the tone.

How can this moment be identified here, at the end of the 90s? Where can we take it, how can we use it? And, most crucially, how can we preserve and protect it?

*I*N FRONT OF ME, A LITTLE DRAMA UNFOLDS: two municipal workers, with a tanker and a long pipe, spritz the sculpture, scrubbing off the graffiti scribbled on it. They struggle helplessly with a big hysterical dog freaked by the water. The dog barks endlessly, grabs the pants of one of the workers, until finally his person manages to pull him away. He doesn't forget until he reaches the far end of the street, turning around repeatedly, shooting last barks of protest at the workers with the pipe.

In a few minutes, the round rusty edges of the sculpture dry out. It is hot. Old fans are activated on both sides of the coffee shop, and the contents of the ashtrays are blown in all directions. People with cellular phones make and receive calls. Action. The bronze wolves bathe in the blinding sun of 1:00 p.m. The rural rust, the rural ploughs in the middle of urban commotion, are stranger than ever. Dorchin erected here an inverted, distorted rural world: nothing in this inverted rural microcosm can move except for the stand on which the sculpture rests.

Looked at closely, the stand resembles a cart moving from place to place, sticking its load in one's face.

This cart arrived here from faraway, from Dorchin's kibbutz.

There is a joyful tension between this heavy, enormous mass of iron and its seemingly easy capacity to become mobile. Here is the show, the animals, the surprise, the circus. In this place, Dorchin's mobile iron circus acquires the taste of a gift: one can touch brutality, without being crushed by it.

Translated from the Hebrew by Emanuel Berman

CONTRIBUTORS

Geoff Dyer lives in England. He won this year's National Book Critics Circle Award in criticism for his book *Out of Sheer Rage: Wrestling with D.H. Lawrence*. The story in this issue is excerpted from his novel *Paris Trance*, which Farrar, Straus & Giroux is publishing.

Yan Geling has published widely in Chinese. Her first collection of stories in English translation, *White Snake*, is being published by Aunt Lute Books. *Celestial Bath* is the story on which the recently released film *Xiu Xiu: The Sent-Down Girl*, directed by Joan Chen, is based.

Shaun Levin is a South African living in London. His fiction has appeared in *Stand*, *The Evergreen Chronicle* and *Kunapipi* as well as in several anthologies.

Jeffery Renard Allen's first story, *Shimmy*, appeared in VENUE 1. Next year Farrar, Straus & Giroux is publishing his first novel, *Rails Under My Back*. His first book of poems, *Harbors and Spirits*, appeared this year. He teaches African American literature and creative writing at Queens College, City University of New York.

Bridgett M. Davis is an independent filmmaker. Her first feature film, *Naked Acts*, has screened in several international film festivals and was named Best Film in the 1996 Berlin International Black Film Festival.

Wayne Koestenbaum is the author of several books of criticism, including *The Queen's Throat: Opera, Homosexuality, and the Mystery of Desire* and *Jackie under my Skin*. Among his works of poetry are *Ode to Anna Molfo and Other Poems* and *Rhapsodies of a Repeat Offender*.

Leo Ou-fan Lee writes frequently for journals in Taiwan, Beijing and Hong Kong. His latest book, *Shanghai Modern*, is being published by Harvard University Press.

Hugo Achugar lives in Montevideo and frequently teaches in the United States. Among his many books of poetry is *Orfeo en el salón de la memoria*, which won Uruguay's national poetry prize in 1991. He has also written several books of criticism and a novella, *Cañas de la India*, under the pseudonym Juana Caballero.

Rubén Martínez is author of *The Other Side* and an editor at Pacific News Service. He has written extensively on culture and politics in Mexico, El Salvador and the United States. He lives in Los Angeles.

Leslie Stainton has written for numerous publications and scholarly journals. *Lorca and Dalí* is excerpted from her new biography of Federico García Lorca, *Lorca: A Dream of Life* (Farrar, Straus & Giroux).

Ronit Matalon teaches literature in Tel Aviv. Her first novel, *The One Facing Us*, was excerpted in *VENUE 3* and has been published by Henry Holt/Metropolitan Books.

Giuliana Maresca is a photographer/musician who has relocated from Los Angeles to Harlem.

WORLD WIDE WEB ADDRESSES
Additional information is also available through the Publisher's web home page site at http://www.gbhap.com. Full text on-line access and electronic author submissions may also be available.

ORDERING INFORMATION
Four issues per volume. 1997-99 Volume: 1.
Orders may be placed with your usual supplier or at one of the addresses shown below. Claims for nonreceipt of issues will be honored if made within three months of publication of the issue. See Publication Schedule Information. Subscriptions are available for microfilm editions; details will be furnished upon request. All issues are dispatched by airmail throughout the world.
SUBSCRIPTION RATES BASE list subscription price (four issues): US $38.00, GB £26.00, ECU 32.00.* This price is available only to individuals whose library subscribes to the journal OR who warrant that the journal is for their own use and provide a home address for mailing. Orders may be sent directly to the Publisher and payment must be made by personal check or credit card.
Separate rates apply to academic and corporate/government institutions. Postage and handling charges are extra.
*ECU (European Currency Unit) is the worldwide base list currency rate; payment can be made by draft drawn on ECU currency at the current conversion rate set by the Publisher. Subscribers should contact their agents or the Publisher. All prices are subject to change without notice.

PUBLICATION SCHEDULE INFORMATION To ensure your collection is up-to-date, please call the following numbers for information about the latest issue published: 44 (0)118-956-0080 ext. 391; 973-643-7500 ext. 290; or web site: http://www.gbhap.com/reader.htm. Note: If you have a rotary phone, please call our *Customer Service* at the numbers listed below.

GENEROUS SUPPORT FOR THE EDITORIAL AND
ARTISTIC PREPARATION OF **VENUE** IS PROVIDED BY

WEISSMAN SCHOOL OF ARTS AND SCIENCES,
BERNARD M. BARUCH COLLEGE,
CITY UNIVERSITY OF NEW YORK.
ALEXANDRA W. LOGUE, DEAN.
ROBERT A. PICKEN, ACTING PROVOST.
LOIS S. CRONHOLM, INTERIM PRESIDENT.